My
Perfect
Mirror

My Perfect Mirror

*Discovering God's Power
and Truth within us.*

ROSALYN U. IKPATT

WESTBOW
PRESS®
A DIVISION OF THOMAS NELSON
& ZONDERVAN

WestBow Press books may be ordered through booksellers or by contacting:

WestBow Press
A Division of Thomas Nelson & Zondervan
1663 Liberty Drive
Bloomington, IN 47403
www.westbowpress.com
1 (866) 928-1240

Scripture taken from the King James Version of the Bible.

ISBN: 978-1-5127-3280-1 (sc)
ISBN: 978-1-5127-3282-5 (hc)
ISBN: 978-1-5127-3281-8 (e)

Library of Congress Control Number: 2016903297

Print information available on the last page.

WestBow Press rev. date: 3/22/2016

Dedication

This book is dedicated to the glory of God in Christ Jesus and His Spirit. It is also dedicated to PJAK, my blessing and reward. God is with you and also in you, now and always. To my family, both by blood and by His grace, you are priceless to me. Thanks Dad!

May the Holy Spirit minister God's perfect love within the minds of everyone who will ever read this book. May He continue to remove every layer of deception, as He reveals Christ, and all that He has purposed for each person; my prayer is that this will change them from the inside out and present them completely in their perfect mirror image in Christ. May His kingdom come in each life, in Jesus's name.

Preface

A good fraction of our self-perception happens in front of a mirror. A mirror provides a priceless opportunity to make great efforts at looking our best, and that means something different for everyone. The goal depends on the various qualities each person's culture, society, and other influences have encouraged him or her to value as desirable. These feed our inherent lack of satisfaction and confidence in who we are and compel us to do anything necessary, if only by appearance, to become who we may want to be. Despite efforts to have a perfect image, we see only form and are still stuck with a superficial and incorrect image.

Welcome to your perfect mirror; in it you see yourself differently than you've ever seen or known. Here you find what is true about you, not what you are told or have been made to believe. But it is what has always been true about you, even before you were born. Nothing can change or alter this truth in any way. You may, however, believe otherwise and miss out on it. Logic calls this perspective foolishness, so we ignore them. Wisdom calls it truth and uses it to overcome.

In a world where the knowledge of God and His truth aren't regarded as sovereign, our natural eyes are very limited in sight because they feed off wrong information we have accepted as truth. We wrongly believe our lives are ours to manage, care for, and provide for independently of God or at best from a distance. We base all things on our ability or the lack of it. The belief system that fails to acknowledge God as our only source in all things is wrong and will manifest a different set of situations than God intended.

This is why Jesus came—so that by His

death and resurrection, He would provide full payment for the various manifestations of our sin of unbelief, which is the basis of all sins. He has removed everything that stood between us and God; we now have access to live in Him, and through His eyes, we would be able to see ourselves and our world clearly. It is a completely different picture, because this sight sees truth as God ordained it to be. It is your perfect mirror image. It is also your only real image, because it shows the blueprint of who you truly are as your maker presented it. This truth automatically debunks everything else you've believed about yourself and your world.

Growing into this unusual-yet-exciting process can be a little challenging, so in His love, God sent us a helper, the Spirit of truth. He helps us to sort through the lies. That fact makes everything else you've ever heard or known about yourself highly questionable. The good becomes better, and the bad is correctly positioned under your feet. This will happen as you allow your mind to be renewed in Him. It is my intention, as His Spirit leads, to share truths that will chip away at the distorted mirror image so the true person within will be revealed.

Be prepared to meet the real you inside and be amazed by the power you have. Paul said in Ephesians 1:19 (KJV) "And what is the exceeding greatness of his power to us-ward who believe, according to the working of his mighty power," The operative word is *believe*. Get excited! There is so much more to discover in Christ.

Introduction

This is my perception of God's opinion of you, a reminder of who you truly are as His child, His temple and His vessel.

I hear His Spirit say to you,

I know you. You can barely recognize yourself, but I see you. You've allowed yourself to believe so many lies about Me, yourself, and others; and these have created a fake world for you. It isn't real. You've never been anything else but a vessel in your earthly presence— My vessel. For so long, you've believed that the power to work and sustain this vessel is you. No, this isn't true. I made you. I made you to be a temple, to be inhabited by My Spirit, as the power and outlet to do My will. You are not your own; you never were. Your body wasn't created for your own ideas and plans but for My Spirit to dwell and carry out My ideas and plans through you. Still you chose wrong. In My Son, Jesus Christ, I paid for your sins after you had gone astray. I paid with My life's blood. I shed My blood, died, and rose again. I did this to reconnect you with Me as your source of an endless life in Me.

Now I have sent my helper, My Spirit who is truth. Let go of anything He shows you as being unnecessary in you. Your old ways cannot be in the way of My work in you. Whatever you hold as true on earth is held as true in heaven as long as you are under the power of My Spirit. You cannot exist as a separate being from Me. My will must be your will, because I am your only source of life. Your union with Me in My Spirit is your lifeline, but be at rest; I am the One keeping you. I'm able to sustain you just by the simple unforced reality of truth. My Spirit in you reveals Me in you. Know that as a part of Me, you have constant help. The essence of who I am continually flows into you, but you need to keep still and believe.

Don't overextend yourself at any time but be very conscious of My power working in you in every situation.

Again I say, you are not your own, and that includes every aspect of your life. I need to enable you to do My work on earth as I purposed. My power is the enabling, and in it is everything that pertains to life and godliness, even as you live in Me. Don't look elsewhere for ability or power of any kind. Within you, in Me, is all you need. Stay ready and open for Me at all times.

With this renewed understanding in mind, I invite you to come with me, as we go on a treasure hunt in each of the following Bible verses. For emphasis and proper application in thought, these themes will be referenced throughout the texts and commentaries. We will enrich our lives even more with God's truth, as we seek to become fully contained in our one and only perfect image, Jesus Christ.

"I will praise thee; for I am fearfully and wonderfully made: marvellous are thy works; and that my soul knoweth right well. My substance was not hid from thee, when I was made in secret, and curiously wrought in the lowest parts of the earth. Thine eyes did see my substance, yet being unperfect; and in thy book all my members were written, which in continuance were fashioned, when as yet there was none of them" (Ps. 139:14–16 KJV).

We must completely understand that we were once only an idea in God's mind, and He created each of us carefully and specifically for a purpose. Your earthly presence started in the mind of God before you were born, so your destiny depends not on where you were born, on whom you were born to, or any other such circumstances. Your life story—with all the things you've never told anyone, all the shame and so-called successes—can find its true manifestation only in Christ, your perfect mirror. You don't need to carry your burdens anymore; your worth is determined not by favorable or unfavorable statistics but by whose you are.

It changes everything for us when we know and fully believe that the truth about us has yet to be fully revealed. In the passage above, David spoke by the Holy Spirit and revealed what God says about each of us. Our origins are traced all the way to Him and His life in us. It is because of this truth that we can strongly declare, with all confidence, that anything else that seems to oppose or negate this fact is false. The words "fearfully and wonderfully made" defy adequate human explanation. No human words or knowledge can properly describe the intricate details of what constitutes the human being. What we currently know is extremely limited, and to think there is a unique design and plan for each one releases a new sense of purpose.

God's Word has its own power. The

information is for us to know and believe; the power of His Word is activated when we believe. God will, by His Spirit, apply His Word in each person's life as is necessary for his or her growth and specific purposes. Let your heart, mind, and soul accept the truth about your real origin.

Break free from the hijacked understanding of what you know so what is true can make way for you and for His kingdom in you. Allow yourself to believe these words today, whatever they may mean to you.

"So God created man in his own image, in the image of God created he him; male and female created he them" (Gen. 1:27).

This verse is overwhelming. No one can fully comprehend being made in God's image. So much is packed into this verse that the best thing is to sit with it for a while and ask the Holy Spirit to knead it into you as necessary.

It was God's idea to make us in His image. Even our sin cannot change that. We may lose out by living in disobedience and being restricted to deception, but we only need to know the truth to be released into the fullness of our image in God as He assigned it to us respectively. We were each created in Christ Jesus unto good works to manifest God's purposes on earth. We have the wisdom of God as part of our godly image.

You are made in the image of the Most High God. This is an exciting adventure to look forward to each day as you become more and more aware of the truth about your true image. As you commune with Him in His Word, by His Spirit, and in worship, this connection will reflect in your relationship with people and issues. Open your mind to receive all He will reveal to you about being made in His image. It's bound to be beyond your best imagination and will exceed your highest inspired thought and perception.

Another way to do that is to read this verse aloud till you hear it again on another level, for the Word of God has its own power. Ask God for that power to fully believe. Ask Him to lay a solid foundation in your heart, redirect your mind to fully accept His truth, and reset your image accordingly. The image of God is in us, and His Spirit will bring it to fullness in us as we yield to this truth.

"And be not conformed to this world: but be ye transformed by the renewing of your mind, that ye may prove what is that good, and acceptable, and perfect, will of God" (Rom. 12:2).

This verse describes one of the reasons why you need to discover your own perfect mirror image. The mirror is Christ Jesus. You shouldn't accept and live out the image you see (and currently know and feel) of yourself outside of Christ, since it is of this world. The real and perfect image is received only by the renewing of your mind. The things you will discover in your renewed mind cannot be described in simpler terms than that they are the good, acceptable, and perfect will of God.

I notice the reference to being "transformed by the renewing of the mind" as a suggestion of an earlier awareness of truth. I believe that if you were asked to introduce yourself, you would go into details about your name, age, occupation, family life, work experience, and many other details that describe you. It's almost natural to omit, excuse, or embellish the gray and unpleasant parts. I believe we do that because we know deep in ourselves that we're capable of being better. It's hard to accept in front of others that we're anything but wonderful human beings. We respond favorably to flattery, even when we know it's used for manipulation or any such deception. We're so needy of affirmation that we'll take it from anyone. These aren't necessarily bad traits; I believe these were our God-given connection points to His love and through Him to others, and our minds need to be renewed to reactivate this within us.

I think these also speak of our inner yearnings, a strong conviction, or maybe a very faint memory that there's something better within our reach. By not conforming to the world, we now are able to yield our thoughts, senses, and all our connection points to God as He purposed. The reference to the world here speaks of, among other things, any order or application of life that is outside the will of God.

It is true that there is something better: Christ within you, your perfect mirror. God wants to reveal it to you even more by His Spirit if you will let Him. A renewed mind in Christ is real, and we can become used to it as our true image.

"Therefore leaving the principles of the doctrine of Christ, let us go on unto perfection; not laying again the foundation of repentance from dead works, and of faith toward God" (Heb. 6:6).

This is a call for growth, and the destination is our perfect image. This image is our proper positioning in Christ for the work of His kingdom in us as He purposed. There are a series of processes and levels of growth that, if ignored, might have us going in circles in the things of God. A close walk with God will depend on a clearer understanding of what the relationship is about and what He expects of us at each place. It isn't enough to just agree that Jesus is Lord, without yielding to the steady and detailed process, of stripping off what became necessary, when we depended on ourselves in error. That is the journey to the revelation of your real image. That is when we learn to see our real selves through a perfect mirror—Christ.

It's easy to fall into this pattern of just going

through the motions of godliness and still feel like you're making progress. Sometimes we even resort to using God as a pacifier, a soft shoulder to lean on long enough for us to bounce back from a challenging situation. Then we go back and continue to live on our own terms—or at best, we just enjoy the inspiration that comes with godliness but don't find it necessary to go in a little more or to make any changes that will reveal our real image underneath all that.

The admonition here is to remind us of the ground that is already covered, with a hint that there is much more to discover in the journey, so there is no need to go in circles. It is different for each person, for you will grow only according to the measure of faith given to you. Our perfect image as found in Christ is revealed in us as we allow ourselves to continue to grow.

"For we are his workmanship, created in Christ Jesus unto good works, which God hath before ordained that we should walk in them" (Eph. 2:10).

This is the primary goal of life: to walk in the good works God prepared beforehand for each of us. The maker had a plan, but we sometimes believe wrongly and are convinced of deception so much that we don't find God's will adequate. Therefore, we make an alternative plan that unfortunately always works against us. This fact may be hard to take in all at once for some, but the truth is that none of those other things that compel us really matter as much. Everything finds its proper place here in the total surrender to God. We were never created as a separate entity of our own to have our own independent ideas and motives outside of Him. All our inabilities have their roots from that erroneous disconnection. That has to change.

We start by consciously turning everything over to God, and we listen for His voice in every situation. There may be things, issues, and relationships that hinder or limit this grand purpose in your life, but starting over with God is simpler than what you imagine. With a heart full of conviction of His grace and love for you, just tell Him you're turning the control and direction of your entire life over to Him and that you will do what you know to be right and obey as He directs. Do that daily and believe He is leading you. Be at peace. The difference will be that the burden of life will be gradually lifted off you and given over to Jesus Christ; He will direct and redirect everything to make room for Himself. You will need to accept the changes as something positive because they really are, and you will be amazed by what He is doing in and through you. You in Christ are a perfect image, and this is completely different from you on your own as a separate and limited being.

You are Christ's, and Christ is God's. Limitations are available only outside of Him. Father, we praise You, for it pleased You to create us in Your image in Christ Jesus, Your Son. Thank You that You have a plan for us. Forgive us for wasting time and energy on other things and trying to function out of our human limitations instead of Your endless grace for us. Let these words become alive in us so Your plans will manifest in us for Your glory in Jesus's name.

"For God so loved the world that he gave his only begotten Son, that whosoever believeth in Him should not perish, but have everlasting life. For God sent not His Son into the world to condemn the world; but that the world through him might be saved" (John 3:16–17).

This familiar verse is our focus here. Sometimes we become so used to certain Bible verses that we miss the life-changing information they carry. Salvation was motivated by love at a time when we were still deep in sin and couldn't tell the difference between good and evil. God sent His Son, Jesus Christ, to die and pay for every punishment of disobedience that was due us so we would walk and live freely in Him. A great rescue has taken place, and thousands continue to receive this awareness every day all over the world. The hands of death have been pried off us, our sin condemned us, but we can now live. It is real. You are so valuable to God; He didn't come in Jesus to chastise you about your sins. He knows you've sinned, and His holiness cannot tolerate sin in any form, yet He loves you enough to do whatever is necessary to disconnect you from sin and bring you back to safety in Him, even when this required Him to suffer and die.

In human terms, imagine floodwater almost sweeping you away. Suddenly, someone risks his own life to pull you to safety. This is a pale comparison, but the threat of perishing is similar. It's a lot better than that because Jesus as the redeemer not only rescues you; He takes on Himself every sin and shame that was supposed to come to you. He provides for your every need; lives in you as your strength, wisdom, and ability; and protects and comforts you. The list is endless. Life without Christ is never an option if you know the truth; He rewards those who diligently seek Him.

Pause and allow God to make contact with your heart and be refreshed of this life-changing love that redirects our lives from a place of perishing to a place of enjoying eternal life. Discover again what God really thinks of you as you ponder what He did and still continues to do for you. You are saved; personalize this truth, own it, and live it. It is the gift of God. Give Him the glory.

Lord, we thank You for Your love. May it be shed abroad in our hearts for Your glory. Make this verse become real in our lives and help us to believe it fully and rejoice in this truth. We have been set free by the same One whom we sinned against. We have been pardoned and received again into our place in Him.

"Giving thanks unto the Father, which hath made us meet to be partakers of the inheritance of the saints in light: Who hath delivered us from the power of darkness, and hath translated us into the kingdom of his dear Son: In whom we have redemption through his blood, even the forgiveness of sins" (Col. 1:12–14).

Our identity in Christ automatically relocates us from the kingdom of darkness, with all its forms of deception and entanglements, and positions us in God's light, where His truth reigns and where all deception and its effects are overcome. Many have neither made a conscious effort to move nor become fully aware of this provision. They have yet to realize that the strength and wisdom of God in Christ have enabled them to live. In Christ you don't get a makeover; nothing false is allowed. Instead you are stripped of your fake coverings and perceptions to reveal the true person, because nothing can change God's original plan in you.

You can choose to ignore it and believe a lie about yourself, but this will be only at a loss to you.

The various frames or perspectives of life that defined us according to sin, according to culture and other temporal issues, are no longer valid. Everything that goes against what God says to be true about us no longer has authority, because we know God's truth. That is what Jesus died and rose again to reveal. He has delivered us and moved us into Himself. The only truth about us is what our maker knows and declares concerning us. It is only when you believe this that you will be empowered to ignore every other deceptive voice that seems real.

We have been relocated from an unfavorable place of error, limitation, and disconnection—to everything that pertains to life and godliness—to a place of mercy, comfort, pardon, ongoing counseling by His Spirit, and restoration. It's important to be fully aware of what Jesus did for us and the benefits that are ours because of it. Even our ignorance can attack this truth, for deception has so burdened and conditioned us. The Spirit of God was given for such reasons to help us every step of the way, and He leads even the most broken and deceived soul back to the safety that is in God in Christ Jesus, His Son and our Savior. Please read the verses aloud to yourself until you feel you've heard them more clearly than you ever have before.

Father, we thank You for Your love for us. We've been received into the kingdom of Your Son, Jesus. May nothing be able to steal this truth from our hearts. Instead may this truth always rise up to conquer every opposing voice. May our entire being be reset to this truth in Jesus's name.

"Seeing that ye have put off the old man with his deeds; And have put on the new man, which is renewed in knowledge after the image of him that created him" (Col. 3:9–10).

Your true life in Christ comes with a new understanding, one that is totally different from what you knew before; there is a renewed knowledge, and the process gradually upgrades you to your original position at creation. You were created in His image, your perfect mirror.

Many have explored (and would be glad to find) an alternative belief system that would negate the one we're currently compelled to live in, but we would rather have life on our own terms. There is no valid will outside of God's will, and all things must be done according to His terms. There is nothing good for us when it isn't in His will. It may feel like a good thing for a while, but we are always left powerless, helpless, and fully controlled by the deceptive ideas and theories that we subscribe to. Like the prodigal son, when you come to Christ, you've returned to your home. God calls you to be more than a thankful servant; you are His child. and He wants to treat you as such. Allow Him to do so. It is your right, as He has so graciously forgiven your sins and made His Spirit available to you to guide you.

Be thankful and confident that He went as far as becoming a man; He lowered Himself to touch and deal with sin, yet He conquered it fully. The law of sin and death couldn't overcome Him because it is beneath Him. Be assured that He really means for you to come all the way home, like the prodigal son, to take off your worn-out clothes, the deceptive things you had put your trust in, and to be clothed in new robes of His truth befitting a son or daughter. There is also more than enough provision of everything you need, for in Christ there is everything that pertains to life and godliness.

Correct your vision accordingly by believing God's truth in His Word and replacing it where you assumed otherwise. God's Spirit in you keeps you in alignment and in the flow of His love. You were made in His image so you are returning to your original place in Him. Rest in Him and rejoice, for henceforth, in your new image, the law of the Spirit of life in Christ Jesus is the only law that directs your life.

"And he said unto them, I beheld Satan as lightning fall from heaven. Behold, I give unto you power to tread on serpents and scorpions, and over all the power of the enemy: and nothing shall by any means hurt you" (Luke 10:18–19).

The One who made heaven and earth from the mere words of His mouth, the same who created you in His image and sent His Son to die for you, is the same who loves you with an everlasting love. He is the only One capable of giving you the only correct information on how to handle life's problems. He says you do have authority to overcome all power of the Enemy. Somehow it's easier to believe everything else but this. Every form of deception has cleverly programmed us and positioned us in every aspect of life to make it seem as if there are no real alternative opinions or solutions to life's issues.

Imagine you are stranded in a desert and

someone tells you he or she knows of a way that you could walk across that desert to safety without heat exhaustion, blisters, or the dangers of creepy and wild animals. What if the solution was just a little ointment you put on yourself and a few words to say as you go along? Most people would try this way. Whenever human beings are overwhelmed or desperate, they are more willing to try something new.

In your true and perfect mirror, Jesus Christ, the One from whom our true reflection shines forth, there is understanding to overcome all lies, but we must decide to identify with the truth than with anything else that tells us otherwise. I can only imagine what changes would be in the world if even ten percent of believers in Christ Jesus believed enough to let His truth manifest in their lives.

We have the authority God has given. Dominion is an inherent ability of a child of God; it isn't something spectacular to attain. It's your right in Christ. He is God, and in

Him all things consist. Own this truth. Believe God. Receive it by recognizing it as real and accessible to you. Use it by bringing it up in your mind with thanksgiving as often as possible until it becomes a natural part of your belief system. Say to yourself, "Christ in me completes everything that was lacking in me, everything that pertains to life and godliness. This is one of the many gifts I receive out of His incomparably great power to us who believe."

God Himself gives you the will to work and do His will. Disconnect completely from anything that defines you as a separate being from Christ, in whom you were created. He is your source of power and authority but only and always for His own glory, for you are part of Him in Christ. His position as God naturally puts everything under Him; if you are in Him, in Christ Jesus, His Son, then you are positioned accordingly. The above verse makes proper sense in this context.

Rejoice. You really, truly, can trample on

serpents and scorpions and be over every power of the Enemy, and nothing shall by any means hurt You.

Thank You for Your faithfulness, Lord. May Your Word give life to us even as You work Your will in us.

"For I know the thoughts that I think toward you, saith the Lord, thoughts of peace, and not of evil, to give you an expected end. Then shall ye call upon me, and ye shall go and pray unto me, and I will hearken unto you" (Jer. 29:11–12).

If some world leader or influential person said these same words to you, your life as you know it would instantly change. Everything and everyone in your life would need to adjust to accommodate the possibilities expressed in this statement. Your present and future plans would be based on this promise. There would be a new spring to your steps and definite actions, which would show your total belief in what was said. The truth is, coming from any human being, no matter his or her scope of influence, these would be just mere words until what is said really happened. Even then, there could be some major or minor changes when the words do happen.

God's promises are more certain. He truly rewards those who diligently seek Him. No one, situation, or natural disaster can stop Him from doing what He promised to do. He created everything; the things He created know and respond to Him, and in Him they all consist.

I have seen people spend money in preparation to move to a different city when all they had was just the promise of a job offer there. I have seen a car company sell a brand-new car to a kid possessing only a job offer letter. Why is it so hard for us to take God at His word? We must consciously choose to believe God as the only truth. As far as humans go, no matter their level of authority, anything can change, because no one is in control of his or her life and circumstances, but God answers to no one but Himself. Nothing stops Him from keeping His promises, and unlike man, He wouldn't just say something for the sake of saying it. Man has a need to brag about what he can do because he is aware of his limits but

God is not limited in any way so He just keeps His promises.

It's okay to fully trust Him. He would like that more than anything, because your perfect image is designed to include that. Our image is in Him; that is when we no longer have or need our own ability because we become able in Him. God's thoughts toward us are those of peace, and they always include a plan and destination that favor us and glorify Him. This truth should put our hearts and minds at ease, and give us joy.

Thank You, Father, for Your care of us. Help us to receive and use it fully for Your glory in Jesus's name. Amen.

"But even the very hairs of your head are all numbered. Fear not therefore: ye are of more value than many sparrows" (Luke 12:7).

I'm so glad God chooses to go to these great lengths to show us how much He cares. Pay attention to the details of this verse. First are numbered hairs: Chances are that neither you nor your father, mother, spouse, or best friend knows the number of your hairs. This isn't a figure of speech. God means exactly what He states here in His Word. This might seem to us to be an unnecessary gesture, but He knows that He created you to be loved and cared for deeply and closely. There might even be a bigger and more divine reason for numbering the hair we are yet to discover. He is God, and He created every part of you according to certain specifications as He particularly purposed in His will for you. He cares and protects every part of you with close attention. He knows you are your real self only when you know His love and depend on it. Your perfect image is found in His love.

He knows that apart from Him you really can do nothing, so He loves you anyway, just as is necessary. He is concerned about the smallest details of your life, even those things you just brush aside. He arranged the cells in your body, and they continually function at His prompt. Science, as wonderful as it is, just shows man's ongoing effort at understanding, but the truth is in Christ, who is the wisdom of God.

Let your maker take care of you. He is very willing and able; if He numbers your hairs, it shouldn't be too hard for you to trust Him. I'm still blown away by the fact that He didn't let us die in our sins but came down to die in our place; this detailed show of unimaginable love should completely confirm the truth about Him. He is trustworthy. No one is above Him, so there is absolutely nothing to fear. In Him all things consist. When you lean on your understanding, you automatically subscribe to a different set of rules, ones that defeat you, for you are not connected to your power source; therefore, you are not in your correct image.

The same One who could have allowed us to suffer the consequences of sin is now making several pleas to us to come back and have life in Him. His love really endures forever. Upgrade your mirror image to include this great love as a place of rest for your mind and a reason to trust Him completely.

"Behold, what manner of love the Father hath bestowed upon us, that we should be called the sons of God" (1 John 3:1).

Everyone instinctively knows to seek and fight for what he or she considers desirable and necessary. Here we are given a free gift. All things seen and unseen, known and imagined, are completely under His jurisdiction. In His love, the Most High God has declared us worthy to be called the sons or children of God. The privileges are endless.

Many of us haven't taken advantage of the perks this comes with. As a believer in Christ Jesus, you should wake up each morning like a prince or princess would, knowing you are a child of God and that your day is set before you. Don't remember yourself each morning as just another human going about his or her business and hoping and praying that God sees you through another day. The issues in your life should be defined according to God's power, not according to your ability or the lack of it.

There is a great difference there; any child who lives with his or her parents is fully aware of the parents' responsibility for him or her; he or she isn't generally anxious about things like shelter, food, and other basic provisions. The child knows he or she is entitled to them and expects them. An orphan would have the exact opposite expectations, unless he or she was fully adopted and made to be a complete member of a family. To be God's child means to be rescued from hopelessness and to be brought back to the original plan of God, positioned again in Him for victory.

He is happy to call us His children, but we should be exceptionally grateful that He does and that He loves us so much even when we don't deserve it. You are His child. Say to yourself, "I am God's child." No one can ever take this identity from you. You can abandon it when you believe lies about yourself, but it will be there, waiting to be picked up again. I don't understand why we would abandon it, but sometimes we fall to temptation. If you compare your situation when you believe truth to when you allow yourself to fall back into your old ways and believe a lie, the difference would make you fight to stay in Him as He reveals more of Himself in you. Remember it often with joy.

There is so much to gain in this recognition as His child. We continue to explore this vast and unfathomable love of God as we seek to be conformed to our perfect mirror image in Him.

"For he hath made him to be sin for us, who knew no sin; that we might be made the righteousness of God in him" (2 Cor. 5:21).

This is a clear and simple picture of our true and perfect reflection. The One whom sin cannot attack or defeat, our sinless Jesus, has fully taken our place. He has taken all our sins on Himself and destroyed them at the cross. We who have received this gift of forgiveness and repentance are now fully identified by His righteousness. This is the difference between life and death in every sense. When we aren't able to make use of this free offer, we are reduced to our own strength and ability, and we all know they are never enough. We also begin a downward spiral, which doesn't lead us to life

The life of God is made available to us in this gift; it is the life we were created to live. Don't be afraid of what is rightfully yours; you were created to have full ability because your every existence is and should be an extension of God's power and ability. You live and move and have your being in Christ; that is the only thing to know about yourself, and you should never perceive yourself any other way

I notice that people camp outside a store in the early hours of the day when there is a big sale going on. Some people are willing to camp out overnight in the cold, if need be. Most people appreciate any reprieve they can get from the cost of the things they need and will make any adjustments to accommodate any inconvenience that comes with doing that. There is an inner knowing that we are somehow trapped and that things could be better, so we subconsciously look to take advantage of any little crack in the wall that seems to hole us in.

Again here is the good news; Jesus took all your sins and their consequences. We are covered in His righteousness and wrapped in His love. I pray that you will see this fact to be true in every way. Let Him love you and slowly peel away the layers of self-dependence from you as you enjoy your new life in Him as a reflection of your perfect mirror.

"The angel of the Lord encampeth round about them that fear him, and delivereth them" (Ps. 34:7).

This is a picture to burn into your mind if you fear the Lord. The fear of the Lord is an overwhelming awareness of His righteousness, sovereignty. and total preeminence in all things and beings. This awareness helps us to stay in obedience, because we've come to know Him as truth and see no need to believe a lie; therefore, we fear any possibility of living outside His will. God promises to encamp His angels around you to deliver you. You have your own personal and God-enabled bodyguards. There is a difference between believing and just being excited about the possibilities.

If you've received Him into your heart and made Him Lord of your life, then you fear Him; you are cautious to stay within His will, and you've received His love. It is your right to be protected and helped. God provided that assistance in Jesus for you as part of your normal life in Christ. Despair, worry, and anxiety are strange concepts to God's original plan in us. Many may find that statement absurd and strange, but it's true.

Just as an airplane pilot can never include a possible run-in with a tree at a high altitude in his list of concerns, God is higher than any reason for despair, worry, or anxiety, so there is no way that His plans for us would include those emotions. If an airplane pilot ever gets caught in the branches of a tree, chances are that he or she was flying way too low. It is the same with us who were made in God's image; we were created to be loved, protected, and cared for in every possible way. Any emotion that would suggest anything else would indicate a shift in our positioning in Him.

Bring this truth to the forefront of your mind until it begins to mean more than just a Bible passage. The full intention is for you to become conscious of God's angels encamped around you to deliver you. Let this truth cancel all fears and worries as you move on confidently, knowing that you are enclosed in God's love, even when everything around you seems to suggest otherwise. The truth will set you free. That is a major shift in your perception. Images and emotions that disturb your peace may never be part of your life again and that would be in line with your correct mirror image.

Lord, we thank You that You love us so much that You would provide us with the ultimate security detail. If God be for us, who can be against us? Blessed be Your name in Jesus's name.

"Be not afraid, only believe" (Mark 5:36).

Those are five powerful words. Your understanding outside of Christ deceives you and gives you reasons to fear. These reasons are valid and rational within your scope of understanding. They could be as real as impending danger or an ongoing physical pain. Jesus says not to be afraid but only to believe. He doesn't see defeat in any situation, for in Him all things consist. Fear, a vivid imagination of impending doom, automatically activates our defenses. We instinctively know to find ways to protect ourselves from the danger fear projects to us. Our imagination runs wild, but what information are we using? Is it the truth of God or the lies of the Enemy? We may be more accustomed to the sequences of deception so much that the truth of God, even when we know and quote it, has no place to take root and change things in our lives.

There is a clear indication in this passage of

what our limits are when we aren't in Christ. The problem is that we wrongly believe our limits also limit God; it becomes almost impossible for us to even imagine how God can do what we cannot. At best we trust Him to have more power than we do, but we still see the things we fear as a mighty feat that may require us to help Him.

God's truth doesn't take the seeming severity of our circumstances into consideration. He operates as He is; over and above all we can ask or imagine. He knows it is almost impossible for us to think or imagine above what we see and know, so He tells us just to believe. Believing is the first step to discovering the reality of God's truth. Believe God.

The power of God isn't just inspirational; it is real. Upgrade your mirror image to go past your limits. He goes in you and with you. He is also around you and works through you. Limits don't exist in Him. It is God who works things out in you, and He is able in every circumstance.

"But unto every one of us is given grace according to the measure of the gift of Christ" (Eph. 4:7).

You have the right amount of grace for what God created you to do on earth. Each person has been apportioned grace to help every step of the way. God remembers that we are dust.

A car is made up of a combination of metal, plastic, fiberglass and other substances. When fully built, it is perfect, and every intricate detail is put in place, from the highly technical to the basic utilities, such as cell phone charging slots, cup holders, anything that will make the car convenient for the driver. The car, however, isn't put to full use until someone drives it or somehow mans it.

We are dust, just a pack of human flesh operating in the residual power that holds the earth together, but in Christ, in His love, He has equipped every person with the fullness of ability to live as He has planned for him or her to do. His grace always works in you in reference to where He created you: in Christ. You possess it in you, and you discover it when you believe in Him.

Include this truth in your consciousness as you gratefully realize that you have help that is specially tailored to fit into your only real life in Christ. Competition, jealousy and efforts to outdo another, become the undesirable things they really are, when we discover that each of us has adequate grace and faith, to become who we were created to be. Everyone thrives from within by His Spirit to manifest his or her portion of the kingdom on earth. I don't know why you would want to continue to wander around in uncertainty, when the King of Kings lives in you by His Spirit as your help.

Your share of grace is waiting on you to live out your unique measure of the gift of Christ. There are many whose lives and purposes are directly attached to your specific measure of gift because we are connected to help each other grow. Do your part in the kingdom; you were born and equipped for this. It is the core of your perfect image, purpose, and destiny.

Lord, help us to adjust our image according to the grace that has been given to us. We thank You for this gift and yield ourselves to You to fully activate it for Your glory. In Jesus's name, amen.

"For to be carnally minded is death; but to be spiritually minded is life and peace" (Rom. 8:6).

This is a call for adjustment. The truth doesn't suggest ideas; it declares what works, because anything else would be false. Being carnally minded is being fleshly minded and is in total opposition to the life we receive from God through Jesus. The Bible also says the flesh profits nothing, but the Spirit gives life.

The carnal mind refers to the parts of our lives that aren't yielded to God through Jesus and by His Spirit in us. Everything in our lives that doesn't come from a place of belief and confidence in the power at work within us draws strength from another source that is opposed to God. This is an active part of us by error; it is the reasoning that validates the world we created when we believed a lie, and it is also the result of trusting in ourselves and others rather than in God. Since it is limited, it judges and processes everything incorrectly.

To invest heavily in something so inherently wrong and totally depend on it, cannot lead to anything else but death, both spiritually and physically. When we live outside our intended place, we become positioned away from our provisions and are denied the things that are our God-given rights.

Now let's look at the other side of the coin: what God offers isn't new; it was that way since creation. We were created in Christ Jesus unto good works, which God has ordained that we should walk in them. Jesus came to rescue us when we detoured from this plan. It was never His intention for us to live outside of Him, since we were created to live in Him by His Spirit within us. When we are reconnected to God, we are able to receive from Him. Life and peace are our normal state.

As we live in our normal state, we automatically turn away from the consequences of sin, which are death and separation from God. May this turning away put us in our perfect image in Him.

"Herein is our love made perfect, that we may have boldness in the day of judgment: because as he is, so are we in this world" (1 John 4:17).

Take a deep breath on the last part of this one: "As he is, so are we in this world." That is what God's love has made perfect in us. Ponder the possibility of this statement being completely and totally true. Now compare it with what you currently believe about yourself and your God-given abilities as a child of God. It's now easy to see what a distorted mirror image we have been holding onto as truth. If the above is true, which it is, then there is no reason for us to suffer at all. What may be referred to as suffering has its sting only because we approach it without God's power. We are fully equipped in Him to handle whatever may come at us; trials don't always need to be easy.

Jesus didn't walk around scared. He wasn't worried about anything because within Him was authority all things acknowledge. Since we were created in Christ Jesus unto good works, we are a part of Him. It would make sense that we are natural partakers in what and who He is. It is in our yielding to Him that we become who we really are. This calls for us to become less conscious of ourselves apart from God and more aware of our lives in Him.

He makes it clear that we can function correctly only within Him when He says in His Word that we can do nothing apart from Him. Those things that seem miraculous are normal for God, and He wants us to know that He created us to live normally in Him. It is our separation from Him as our source that defeats us and renders us unable. I think it's time to rethink our entire existence and let His Spirit renew us accordingly.

Lord, we thank You for these treasures in Your Word. Thank You that You've made every possible way for us to come back and live triumphantly in You. Please enable us as we seek to be all You say we can be; it would be disastrous for us to have had all these gifts and abilities from You since Calvary and still not be able to grow into them. As You are Lord, so are we in this world. Your truth towers above all lies. Blessed be Your name in Jesus's name.

"That in every thing ye are enriched by him, in all utterance, and in all knowledge; Even as the testimony of Christ was confirmed in you" (1 Cor. 1:5–6).

The main purpose for writing this is so you can know the truth about you and have the true image of yourself within and without at all times. Here we are reminded of God's special grace of enrichment in our lives. Our words have weight and substance when they come from this place of enrichment by Him; they would automatically do His will, heal, and give life to us as we say them and to others as they hear it. We would have no need or desire to do otherwise. It is so profound just to imagine that we are enriched in everything. Thankfully we can do better than to imagine it; we can attain it because Jesus paid for it at Calvary.

There is help to do better than we are doing now in everything. We are also enriched in all knowledge, which influences our actions and responses to life.. I can see how this is hard to process, since most of us believe that there is valid and legitimate knowledge outside of Christ. True knowledge is available to us only in Christ. We need to go to God first, and then it will be easy to see how everything else we currently call "knowledge" fits into that. Jesus has qualified us for His knowledge and it is available as we become aware and ask for it.

Lord, help us to believe You and avail ourselves of this great gift of Yours to us. May we not gloss over it as one of those nice promises we like and are thankful for, but may we actually stop, think on it, and open our hearts to receive and let it become who we are in You. This is part of the package of abundant life You shed Your blood for us to receive, our true life in You. In Jesus's name, amen.

"For what man knoweth the things of a man, save the spirit of man which is in him? even so the things of God knoweth no man, but the Spirit of God. Now we have received, not the spirit of the world, but the Spirit which is of God, that we might know the things that are freely given to us of God" (1 Cor. 2:11).

There are two great clues here, the information is as follows: You need to have God's Spirit in you to know the things of God. This is where we miss the mark a lot of times; we sometimes believe in error that we can know the things of God because we can read and hear the Word of God. Thankfully, it has been translated into as many languages, forms, and media as possible. The truth remains that the amazing power of these words are revealed only by His Spirit; the best they can be are mere awe-inspiring words until we receive His Spirit within us as our help.

The second clue here is that God freely gives to us other things, much more than we can ever imagine, but they can be discovered and received only through His Spirit, who knows the deep things of God. We need to see our need to have them in our lives and yield to Him, as they are revealed to us and we are enabled accordingly.

This fact should make any believer excited. The burden of life is lifted when you have help of any kind; it is fully lifted when the central part of who you are is positioned in your only life source, Jesus Christ, and His Spirit keeps you. It is the way God has ordained to work in and through His people. Now please let Him take you past the excitement of knowing about His goodness to the fullness of living and walking in this truth. He will do it if you ask. What other reason would He have to tell you of His goodness if He wasn't going to give it to you? This is what He has always wanted for you: you in Him as your perfect image.

Thank You, Father, for Your overwhelming love for us. Blessed be Your name.

"Be careful for nothing; but in everything by prayer and supplication with thanksgiving let your requests be made known unto God; and the peace of God, which passeth all understanding shall keep your hearts and minds through Christ Jesus" (Phil. 4:6–7).

Worry, care, and anxiety are clear indications of man's limitations. The general reasons for these happen when we depend on our own understanding and find it insufficient to meet our needs. Everyone knows that we don't always have all the answers; neither can we fully control or even understand things around us. The futility of anxiety is clearly shown in the fact that it does nothing to solve the situation, but still it remains the response of us humans to difficult situations.

Our desired cure for anxiety would be a solution to the reason of anxiety, but God says not to be anxious at all. This is quite a stretch to our understanding because we are continually reminded of our limited ability. The admonition of a loving father to us isn't to worry or be anxious. Many may wonder why He would say that instead of just supplying the need or fixing the situation that caused the anxiety, since He is God and can do all things.

God reminds us again that we are not our own, but we belong to Him. If we believe and yield our lives and circumstances to Him, they will be removed from our care and given to Him. When this happens, as always was His plan, we will have no need to be anxious. The things that cause anxiety in our lives don't even come on God's radar as a problem. He is God, and He is all able, all knowing, and all wise. The removal of our burden of anxiety releases His peace within us; with it comes a sound mind and wisdom to sort out the difficulties as He directs. Often we find out that these situations were mere conclusions of error on our part. This would be a big tweak in our mirror image as we get closer each day to our original image in Him.

"According as his divine power hath given unto us all things that pertain unto life and godliness, through the knowledge of him that hath called us to glory and virtue: Whereby are given unto us exceeding great and precious promises: that by these ye might be partakers of the divine nature, having escaped the corruption that is in the world through lust" (2 Peter 1:3–4).

This is one of those highly celebrated Bible verses for me personally. It encapsulates what Jesus did for us. This is the complete package that gives us the ultimate image change. The gift here contains "everything that pertains to life and godliness"; nothing is missing. We receive it through the knowledge of Him who called us by glory and virtue. This knowledge is acquired as the work of God's Spirit in us reveals Jesus Christ in us. The revealing includes the removal of anything that became necessary by error and the rebuilding of broken parts. The unfruitful parts get pruned to allow for growth. Some of the gifts we receive in this process are in the form of promises; the writer in excitement, having had a mere glimpse of them, refers to them as "exceeding and precious promises."

These promises propel us as we learn by His Spirit to believe and trust; they guide our paths as they unfold before us. We receive comfort and sustenance from them in strange and scary moments, but we go on. We are being weaned of the lies we had believed, so everything is new and unusual, but His promises keep us balanced and safe. The ultimate goal is our redeemed image, our perfect image, our divine nature.

Rejoice in this gift and take courage in His love during the process, which will certainly have you on cliff-hanging situations as often as necessary. Remember that you have help, so don't panic when you reach your limits. It has become a resting place where He takes over. Learn to enjoy it, and soon you will forget the meaning of limitations, for you will know that they are functional only when you don't know, have, or trust in your God-given help.

The salvation plan isn't intended only for knowledge; it isn't just for preaching so you would be known as a great preacher or wonderful Christian. It is for living it out for God's glory and in His love; it is also for you personally. This is the corrected version of life as you would want it. You were created in His image with a divine nature. That is your perfect image.

"For all have sinned, and come short of the glory of God; Being justified freely by his grace through the redemption that is in Christ Jesus" (Rom. 3:23–24).

Praise God for this truth. You who have received Him as Savior are included in the group of the justified; you are in a right standing with God freely and by His grace. Say that again to yourself and hear and receive it like you would if you were given an unbelievably nice compliment. This is better than a compliment; Jesus made this truth real and active in your life, and that is the information the verse is giving you. What you should do with this information is believe it. The benefits of being in a right standing with God cannot be overemphasized. It is the difference between your misinformed mirror image and the renewed perfect one.

Your current status in Christ qualifies you for every good thing. It is the reason for your boldness in His presence. You are acknowledged in all realms as His. Everything that was your direct responsibility is now God's direct responsibility. I will repeat that for emphasis. Everything that was your direct responsibility becomes God's direct responsibility as you are hidden in Him.

When you rest in this gift of God, your body is released from care and the consequences of stress. It is better disposed for Him to use it to accomplish the tasks set for you to do. Notice that this is no longer your limited power in you. It is God, and He isn't limited. You can accomplish so much more, but it will be without stress because you are free from fear of failure or incompetence. God in you is above failure and incompetence.

It is wise to note that God doesn't do your will. He will do only His will. You will have difficulties if you try to yield to God only to advance your own plans. There really isn't any plan outside of His. All other plans are just distractions of the Enemy. They will eventually prove themselves to lead nowhere. May His joy come alive in you in a bigger dimension as these truths become situated and function fully within you. Your perfect image awaits.

"Likewise reckon ye also yourselves to be dead indeed unto sin, but alive unto God through Jesus Christ our Lord" (Rom. 6:11).

This is the mind-set that completely overcomes the world. In His Word, God practically begs us to come back to our place in Christ. Different angles and views are presented, but the central message is the same. God has done everything necessary for mankind to come back into full union with Him in Christ as He meant it to be. At every opportunity, He offers a strategy, a parable, a comparison—whatever will drive home His central point. He realizes we are stuck in the details, debating that law and this law. Most times we are so caught up in doing the things of God in our own power and justifying them as godliness. Most times our desire to please God is genuine, but it is nothing but burdensome without Him as the guide and help.

Here we are given a chance to catch a glimpse of what life in Christ is like. In essence, this is saying to just delete what doesn't belong, and what is left is exactly how it should be. Just refuse to bring memories of your life outside of Christ into your mind anymore, as you've come to know the truth about you and God; your former understanding and thought patterns are no longer needed. Resent them, refuse them, and be very terrified to continue to be a part of that sequence of thoughts and belief system.

He has offered forgiveness, which you've received or should receive; use it to its full extent. Let Him do all that is necessary to make you fit for a union with Him again. This will free you to become alive unto God and be used and sustained of Him as He always wanted. An unbroken fellowship with God in Christ Jesus is your perfect image.

"For the law of the Spirit of life in Christ Jesus hath made me free from the law of sin and death" (Rom. 8:2).

This truth is very important. It is very easy to be free and not be aware of it. When anyone has been in a difficult situation for a long time and has come to identify and adjust to the demands and limitations of this condition, such a person must unlearn many things in his or her life after he or she has been freed. Habits acquired during a difficult time don't wear out overnight; they are still predominant in thoughts and reasoning. It takes a good understanding of freedom to discard the bondage that used to be.

The big exchange has happened for us; we have been released from the laws that limited us. Because of sin, we were destined for death and destruction. Our separation from God restricted us from the free flow of His abundance and ever-flowing enabling and provision. We made sense of that and found ways to manage; we did it so much that it became almost impossible to convince us that life could be better than that.

Well, Jesus is here, and we have received Him into our hearts as our Lord and Savior. He brings abundant life to us. He paid for our sins with His life, He shed His blood, and He forgives and washes away our sins. He sends His Spirit to live in us as our guide and helps to fully readjust to our real image and life in Him.

It makes perfect sense to say that the law of the Spirit of life in Christ Jesus has set us free from the law of sin and death. It really has, and we need to let this truth replace every lie we have believed concerning sin in our lives. This is a very profound and deep declaration. This law of life transcends all natural laws and is the basis of miracles and a life of continuous victory in Christ. We have His perfect image.

"For the preaching of the cross is to them that perish foolishness; but unto us which are saved it is the power of God. For it is written, I will destroy the wisdom of the wise, and will bring to nothing the understanding of the prudent" (1 Cor. 1:18–19).

This is a sad Bible verse for me, because of the reminder that a lot of people are actually perishing in the midst of this great love. Many people don't see the sense in the cross of Jesus; others accept it but don't exactly know what to do with it, and they don't see any use for it except maybe as something wholesome to identify with. Some just ignore it as one of those things, while some can tell you the message with so much passion but have no clue as to the power it has.

The message of the cross is the light that pierces through a dark world to give it hope and bring everything to its original state, which is to eventually restore it to the fullness of life.

If this isn't your central perception and belief system, then the cross will be foolishness to you, even if you believe. You will ignore it, debate it, and use the cross as an idol (something to worship and revere or to use for protection) or jewelry.

The suffering, death on the cross, and resurrection of Jesus Christ were necessary to destroy sin and its hold on everyone and everything. To the carnal-minded person, the world as it is, is his or her ultimate reality. The person cannot imagine anything other than the sequence of events that he or she has come to learn as being true and real. Questions and comparisons become unnecessary because this mindset has already accepted this reality as truth. Most just want to know more about this reality, and it is hard for them to see that life exists in a purer form than what they know and that everything else is just a repackaging of the same vicious cycle of unfortunate events.

With this understanding, they would never

appreciate Jesus and His saving grace. The cross would be to them yet another coping mechanism for the weak. Thank You, Lord, that we are weak enough to receive real strength, for in our weakness our God is strong for us. In our desperation we find true life and joy. We discover the maker and keeper of all things when nothing else will do. The cycle of deception wouldn't suffice; we sensed there had to be more, and there was more. This truth really destroys the wisdom of the wise and brings the confined understanding of the prudent to nothing. Life in Christ through the cross and perfect substitution, sacrifice, and love—in them we find our perfect image in Him.

"For as in Adam all die, even so in Christ shall all be made alive" (1 Cor. 15:22).

This is yet another angle to this great love and sacrifice, all provided in an effort to convince you to receive it, walk in it, and be available for His use and sustenance. With the first man, Adam, came the sin of disobedience, which infected the world with sin and separated man from his life source. The reference to death is the continuous deterioration of the human situation because of our disconnection from God, resulting in the chaos and confusion that characterizes life, nature, and everything on earth.

The order of God is simply the submission of all things and lives to Him. Everything finds it proper use in Him. He is the source of it all, for He created all things. Drawing strength from any other source but the truth will find everyone and everything shortchanged and malfunctioning at many levels. Ignoring

God's salvation in Jesus is like a newborn baby choosing to raise and take care of himself or herself without the mother. That choice isn't even available, but we believe we have that option. The same One who made us is the same One who extended Himself in His Son, Jesus. He died and rose again to bring us back to Himself after we went astray in Adam.

A new way was made, and we are able to come back and be strong again. We have tasted good and evil, and we know what we want now. We gratefully choose life in Christ and fully reject death in Adam. Thank You, Jesus, for clothing us with Your righteousness and making us worthy of You again. We have life. We have life in You! Blessed be Your name.

"There is neither Jew nor Greek, there is neither bond nor free, there is neither male nor female: for ye are all one in Christ Jesus" (Gal. 3:28).

I am excited because of the many different ways God continues in His Word to shape our perfect image. Every piece of His Word adds, removes, tweaks, and shapes to remake us into our perfect image in Him. In Christ, we aren't recognized or identified in ways we have come to know of ourselves. Nationality, gender, social position, and those things that divide and categorize us aren't recognized.

The reason is simply because Christ isn't divided. He is the head, from whom all body parts, His people, join together to form His body. Without our full knowledge of our perfect image, we are left without the full flow of our source of life, which is the network of God's life in us and others. It flows in unison with others; this is quite a sharp contrast to the individualistic existence we have all come to know and accept as normal life. Separation from God and other people or mostly praying for individual provisions is a mistake, because God supplies all things to His creation in unison; Self dependency distorts our ongoing flow of care and provision from God and creates lack.

When we allow the love of God to be shed abroad in our hearts so much that the walls of division become connection points, through which the joint supply of what is different from the other is allowed to flow, we will become a force to reckon with for what is true about us, and God's kingdom will fully manifest.

We were made to complement each other like the pieces of a puzzle. Just as a missing piece of a puzzle or a wrongly placed one would ruin the total picture, we are at a loss when we allow anything to divide and label us. Everything about each of us was carefully crafted to fit our positioning in the body for the general good. The big picture is that of a body with many diverse parts and specific functions held together by the head, Christ, from whom all life, well-being, and wisdom flow.

Your perfect image is in union with God and others.

"So we, being many, are one body in Christ, and every one members one of another" (Rom. 12:5).

This is the frame or support system that keeps us in balance in Christ. It is a network of how God positioned each of us in Christ for good works. With this in mind, we know and operate within our bearings, our assigned measure of faith, and our callings without jealousy or competition as everyone does his or her part individually but in unison and for a common goal.

The human body must be understood as a single unit with many parts for it to function properly. There are no unnecessary parts in the body. As I'm sitting here, typing, my entire body is involved according to each one's use and capacity. My fingers seem to be the busiest parts right now, but my mind is equally busy. My feet know their contribution is to just be on the floor. My knees know they need to stay bent; my eyes know how important it is that they work with my mind and my fingers in unison. Many other parts seem dormant, but if they were out of working order in any way, this whole typing wouldn't be possible.

This passage helps us to understand what God is doing and how He planned life for us in relation to other believers. They are not separate individuals but different parts of the same body. Each believer depends on others to survive and grow into his or her full potential. There are no other ways to achieve this union but to do it as God planned it. You need to know how you fit into the kingdom and how your purpose contributes to the kingdom of God. You also need to know and see the need for others to come into their respective places in the kingdom. You will be more effective when you operate within your gifts with a full understanding that the fullness of life for the whole body depends on the growing of others into their gifts.

You will be more tolerant of others; you will pray more for their well-being and spiritual strength than you accuse or rebuke them. This verse is information that puts a new perspective in our walk, and beautifully changes our image to fit into our own place in the kingdom, while making room for others to do the same. It births the love that marks us as His own. Our perfect image looks glorious from here.

"I thank my God always on your behalf, for the grace of God which is given you by Jesus Christ" (1 Cor. 1:4).

Grace, by definition, positions the giver, God, as all powerful and all able, not rendered incompetent by sin but also not condoning or tolerant of it in any way. He offers the receiver, us, grace, mercy, and forgiveness as a way out of the mess of sin. He is waiting with open arms to clean, heal, and restore His life to the unbeliever. That gesture by itself is a description of ultimate power. Nothing He does for us takes away from Him. Rejoice. This is what we have in Christ; it is inexhaustible and all-encompassing grace and mercy.

The human mind without Christ cannot fully understand this fact. Like other spiritual things, they seem to be foolishness in perception and a sign of weakness in practice. People who have this state of mind are conscious of a desperate sense of limitation, resulting in an overwhelming need to protect self against a possible shortage or other forms of inabilities. Fear becomes an accepted emotion, exposing the grave condition of the unbelieving mind and the need for God's love and forgiveness.

God's love and guidance are overwhelming and ever flowing in our lives; the light He shines on our path as we walk with Him reveals Him as God in comparison to anything else we believe. What we have in Christ Jesus cannot be exhausted; it keeps unfolding in us till we truly know we don't belong to ourselves; we belong to Him. This is another level of ease when we freely give Him our bodies, His vessels, to use; and the manifestation of His power in us is often mistaken as coming from us. We do well to correct that impression and point people back to Christ. Thank You, Lord, for Your inexhaustible grace.

No one can dare to chart a pattern of God's love shown in His grace to us; it is beyond us, His creation, to follow or try to make sense of it.

Fortunately, all He wants is for us to make full use of it, not to try to fathom it.

Again I say rejoice, for this is available to you and is in you in Christ Jesus. Ask God to activate the favor and spiritual blessings for your specific purpose as you stay close to Him in obedience and grow from grace to grace in your perfect image in Him.

"And that because of false brethren unawares brought in, who came in privily to spy out our liberty which we have in Christ Jesus, that they might bring us into bondage" (Gal. 2:4).

The danger here is the possibility of becoming bound again after we have become aware of our freedom in Christ, and it is always others who convince us again to be bound. Here the Bible identifies such people as false brethren. They profess to be followers of Jesus Christ, but their actions don't support their claims. Their conduct works against the freedom He represents. Christ has made a way for us through His broken body and shed blood. This was satisfactory for the removal of all sins and the cleansing, healing, and restoration. There is no need to be conscious of laws anymore, for the law was completely satisfied in this sacrifice of Jesus. We walk through to the next level of life in Christ, the life made available by the full payment for our sins.

It would be disastrous to go back and try to pay attention to laws when what the law was creating is already available for use. It is comparable to a recipe and the dish. What if for years you strictly followed a recipe to cook a dish, but a professional cook offered you his services and just presented you with an already-made dish of the same recipe? That would cut out the cooking for you. No cooking necessary.

How would you react to this gesture of love and help? Would you just eat the food, or would you want to receive the food with thanks but go ahead and use the same recipe to cook your own dish? It wouldn't make a lot of sense to go back to the recipe when a professional chef cooked the dish and made it available for eating. I wonder why it's so easy for us to be deceived and deprived of the privileges of the complete work of Christ on the cross on our behalf.

Just like in the analogy above, it is a matter of decision to upgrade from recipe cooking to just eating; our part now is obedience and surrender to God, who can make us who He wanted us to be from the start. This true image of us is within and waiting for us to discover it. We must be diligent to stay in our freedom—not as a challenge but because that is the only true source of life and our perfect image.

"But he that is joined unto the Lord is one spirit" (1 Cor. 6:17).

Jesus is the link through whom we have an everlasting flow of His Spirit in us, making us to be of the same Spirit. This exchange can never leave us the same; it changes us to be like we were at creation, in His perfect image within and without. The power released in us as His temples is restorative; it works in us to remove every unnecessary attachment that kept us from the life of God in us. Many would be okay with a little help from God at difficult times while doing their best to handle situations by themselves most of the time. Some actually believe that is the right thing to do, but that would still translate to living below their capacity in Christ.

We cannot come this close to the Most High and still deprive ourselves of the very essence of what our souls need: the freedom and authority of a union with God. We were designed to have one spirit with Him; even when we broke away in sin and error, He came for us to bring us back, not to deal with us from afar.

When Jesus walked on earth, He always said He did what He saw His Father do, and He said what He heard His Father say. That means He was and still is one spirit with the father. We cannot be joined to the Lord and still have a separate life from Him; we must do His will because His Spirit within us would enable us. We can override the promptings of the Spirit by insisting on our own will or by being so burdened by other things that we cannot see or hear what the Lord's Spirit says to us or does. This would be our loss.

Release yourself from the responsibility of independence from God and enjoy the freedom of His righteousness, peace, and joy. His Spirit lives in you. Remember that and live in the victory He accords you. It is your true and perfect image. Rejoice in the Lord.

"Be still, and know that I am God: I will be exalted among the heathen, I will be exalted in the earth" (Ps. 46:10).

The magnitude of this authoritative declaration is usually lost in our panic mode. We cling to it as a last resort when all other fake and powerless things have failed us. What if we knew and understood life along the lines of this clear statement from the only One who can say it? Yes, no one else can make this claim. It is a resounding proclamation that automatically puts everything else in perspective. There is so much power and ability embedded in this. All the universe and beyond know this truth; even the demons know it and tremble.

I think the weight of this statement rests on the declaration in the three words: "I am God" John gave an account of the betrayal and arrest of Jesus shortly before His crucifixion. The soldiers had found Him with His disciples, and they stated that they were looking for Jesus, to which He replied, "I am he." Immediately, for some inexplicable reason, these fierce, strong, and fearless soldiers suddenly drew back and fell to the ground.

Everything in creation acknowledge this truth and respond accordingly. They know who made them, keeps them, and provides for them. They acknowledge His sovereignty. We whom He died for seem to be the least of all creation to become aware of this truth in reality. As human beings, we depend so much on the words of any professional or expert in any certain field of knowledge. We take his or her word as truth because we are convinced that the person knows and is able in every way as far as his or her area of expertise is concerned. We take the doctor's word as law and build our lives around it.

God Almighty reminds you today. In essence He says to you, "I am He who made the heavens and the earth and everything in it. I uphold you, everyone, and everything by the power of My Word, Jesus, My Son, who was made flesh for your redemption. There is nothing that isn't under Me and subject to My power. Just because situations and things are hard for you to understand or fix doesn't mean this fact is the same with Me. I do what I want and how I want it; I take orders from no one, and I love you. So be still."

That is the image you were created to live in, and it is yours to have.

"Thy word is a lamp unto my feet, and a light unto my path" (Ps. 119:105).

Word and *lamp* are not generally interchanged in any sentence, but here *word* is said to be a lamp and a light. In here is hidden the deliverance from the captivity in the minds of many believers in Christ. This doesn't say that "the memorization of Your Word is a lamp unto my feet"; neither does it say, "The preaching of Your Word is a lamp unto my feet." There is only one thing to do with the Word: believe it. It must be preached, and memorizing it helps, but until you believe it, its power will not be available to you. If I asked someone to come to me, he or she would probably just walk to where I was. I wouldn't expect anyone to just stand there and become joyful that I had asked him or her to come to me. The person certainly wouldn't recite, repeat, or memorize what I had said. When we believe, we take relevant action.

The Word of God is information. It is the only true and correct information because Jesus is the truth. He is the truth, because through Him all things were made; everything consists in Him. Nothing exists outside of this truth. Any claims to anything else will show themselves to be false when they all time out and the truth of God in Jesus Christ by His Spirit still stands.

The lies we have allowed to be used as building blocks for our fake existence outside of Christ, are nothing but very clever angles of deception. The only way we can see our way around these very convincing lies is by the illumination God's Word brings to our hearts. His Word tells us what things really are, and as we listen and obey, it becomes our guide out of this maze of deception.

Yes, His Word is sometimes confusing and simply beyond our reasoning or ability to comprehend any aspect of it. This is because His ways are higher than our ways, and all we need to do is know that He loves us and become fully aware that we have absolutely no option to this amazing love, because everything else is a lie. This is how to walk on a lighted path. His Word leads us, and we just trust and obey. He also helps us every step of the way by using His Spirit in us. The destination is for your perfect image to be manifested in Him for His glory.

"These things I have spoken to you, that in Me you may have peace. In the world you will have tribulation; but be of good cheer, I have overcome the world" (Job 16:33).

In this verse we see God in His wisdom making a statement of fact to His children. It is an encouraging word, an explanation and comfort for a weary believer, who may wonder what is happening in his or her life. The stance of this verse is that of One who knows and controls all things. His reference is to keep the believer in immediate peace with a confident promise of a future well-being. There are no implied or subtle apologies here, no indications of self-doubt and uncertainty.

This is hope for the hopeless and solace for the hurting. What a joy to believe and know that events in our lives aren't just random situations, but each is carefully sequenced according to our reactions and other responses to them. His proposed end is for our good. This is all done to fulfill His purposes in us for His glory.

It is good to know that we aren't on our own and at the mercy of the world and all its deception. God has a plan, and when we yield to it, the seeming severity of the situations in our lives loses its sting as we let God instruct us every step of the way. We are able to be partakers of His abundant life, because His plan for us at any time is always a good one.

In believing this, we close our lives to confusion, despair, and anxiety, even in the midst of calamity; and we open them for His joy and peace, which pass understanding. These would really change our mirror image to align with His truth.

"Yea, though I walk through the valley of the shadow of death, I will fear no evil: for thou art with me; thy rod and thy staff they comfort me" (Ps. 23:4).

This is one of those verses most believers in Jesus Christ know by heart. Extreme fear will bring us to find comfort in these words. Here human limitation and God's ultimate ability are compared side by side. For any human, death is a dreaded event, and anything that would put him or her in proximity with even a suggestion of death is strongly opposed.

When life taunts us and exposes our weaknesses and inabilities—and this can happen in sickness, misfortune, loss of any kind, or any unfavorable changes in our lives—our minds are filled with vivid imaginations of what these situations could lead to. Rarely do we imagine good coming out of these situations; we believe wrongly and expect wrong because we become overwhelmed. We can clearly see that we are no match for these calamities, so we fear.

When we remember by His Spirit that we have God in us and He is greater than he who is in the world or in these circumstances, when that becomes included in our reasoning even in the midst of the turmoil, we have access to peace that is real. At this point, we see through a split screen as opposed to being completely overwhelmed with evil, and we know there is power within us. There is grace to acknowledge the hand of God, even in such situations. The only way to move forward is to concentrate on the truth that God is with us and that whatever we seem to face is beneath us.

We can confidently declare—not recite, quote, or chant but declare—that even though we see these things that on their own have potential to defeat us, even to the point of destroying our lives, we also know and have with and within us the ultimate authority. If we can keep our minds on this amazing truth, we could change many things around us and make miracles a common event in our lives. That is our perfect image.

"I press toward the mark for the prize of the high calling of God in Christ Jesus" (Phil. 3:14).

When Paul encouraged himself, his words also encourage and admonish us on this great journey of life in Christ Jesus. The primary focus here is to show you what your high calling is so you can press on toward the goal to win the prize, the prize here being much more than man would ever understand; the true life of God in us is our prize. It is our reality, our perfect image.

Convinced of this truth, we don't wait at every problem; we catch every new day and moment, knowing that we have fresh mercy and grace supplied every morning and moment for our use and for us to give away as the Lord leads us. Forgiveness then becomes an absolute necessity because any alternative would be a distraction, which would mean a hindrance or possible defeat. The time and energy we would spend on rehashing and updating the offenses would keep us from pressing on.

In moving forward, all forms of distraction would be negligible, because we have our entire being set on God's truth concerning us and others. When we know the truth, we forsake all else and go for it. That is the only reaction that shows we have known the truth. One cannot know the truth and remain in deception. Hearing or being inspired by the truth is different from knowing it. The truth takes nothing captive; it simply eliminates all lies by its mere presence.

In our earthly lives, if we must be at a certain place at a specific time for a specific reason, we make every possible effort to ignore or postpone anything else that would keep us from being at that place. Our journey to this place is focused, and our imagination goes before us and helps us to plan for the sequence of events, which involves our reason for the trip. This is such a natural process of the mind that writing it out feels a little awkward in comparison to the admonition to press on toward the mark. Our physical senses know to maintain their truth and therefore are always fully involved in whatever we are doing.

In Christ, we press on by faith, trusting in what the human mind cannot fully process; here we are guided by the voice of a loving shepherd, who continues to instruct us by any means necessary, as the earth and all that is in it are fully His and under His eternal authority. Faith in God through Christ opens us up to be spiritually alert and able to navigate our way into the reality of life offered in Christ. This is our perfect image, which is fully available to you.

"And the peace of God, which passeth all understanding, shall keep your hearts and minds through Christ Jesus" (Phil. 4:7).

It is good to know that God is true and that everything that seems to oppose Him is but lies. The authority expressed in this passage is by itself calming. Here again the gift of God is presented to us as being above anything we could ever imagine, One of the reasons is because God works as God and won't be reduced to the limitations of man. Notice that this peace He offers us automatically scans through every scenario of chastisement from anything and in anywhere, and still it comes out unscathed in that it is said to pass understanding. Imagine the things that would cause you the most anxiety. God's peace can raise you above that in Christ, and it will have no effects on you whatsoever.

It is in the human thought sequence to expect that solutions to difficulties are the only ways to be at peace. We strive to solve our problems instead of depending on God's help and rising above them. Most times we find that problems come in dozens at a time; we just never get any decent breaks from them. They consume us in different ways and taunt us. The real power of anything that chastises us is that it has the ability to steal our peace; when it does, we are opened up for more attacks on our minds and other aspects of our lives.

In Christ, we are aligned higher than the things that would pester us, so even when they seem to be present in our earthly lives, we have an understanding and a witness of His Spirit within that makes the difficulties seem nonexistent. They are, however, training us on how to overcome, and we become more victorious when we master them. Sometimes this witness gives us a solution; sometimes we are just protected from the difficulty involved. Either way, the chaos around us doesn't hold us captive, because the Prince of Peace is our dwelling place. This is the peace that passes human understanding, and it is found only in Christ. Our image in Christ is completely at peace.

"Hold fast the form of sound words, which thou hast heard of me, in faith and love which is in Christ Jesus. That good thing which was committed unto thee keep by the Holy Ghost which dwelleth in us" (2 Tim. 1:13–14).

Paul implored Timothy and us to stay the course of our journey. Again, the heart of God is revealed here. Sometimes I feel like God needs to use "baby talk" to explain things to us. He has used parables, common analogies, and anything that was necessary to help us. He even died on the cross and resurrected again. This shows me how much He wants us to become part of Him again.

I read this passage, and I'm reminded of a father telling his child how to get home from school. He keeps reminding the child to please stay with the directions and keep coming till he or she is at home. One would think that the child would want to go home safely and therefore would naturally follow the directions home. For some, God's Word has yet to become that real, but the central message God shares through this book is one way of showing us who we really are, so we will drop everything else and go home. These are very clear and specific instructions from Paul to Timothy and us; there are subtle suggestions of possible loss, so he admonished us to "hold fast" and "keep." This is a loving road map from God for the journey. He forgives and offers another chance, because He really wants us to come back to our place in Him. It was enough reason for Him to die in our place and rise again.

The parable of the prodigal son would have been a tragic one if the lost son had forgotten all about his former relationship with his father. He knew he had abused his privileges and deserved nothing but punishment, but the memory of his father's love and a good home life before this sin gave him strength to go all the way home and ask for forgiveness.

It is necessary to stay the course of this

journey; there is no option. It may seem like there is one, but whatever isn't real will soon prove itself so. There is only one way; it is Jesus, and He isn't a choice among others. He was the Word at creation and is still the power that holds and sustains the world. He is also the Light of the World. Our perfect image is found only in Christ.

"And because ye are sons, God hath sent forth the Spirit of his Son into your hearts, crying, Abba, Father. Wherefore thou art no more a servant, but a son; and if a son, then an heir of God through Christ" (Gal. 4:6–7).

This has to be one of the most forward jolts we have encountered so far to bring us to our perfect image in God. There is a direct description of exactly how our image is changed. It is only by His Spirit. In our false image, we are unable, because God's Spirit has been ignored in error, but as we reclaim our sonship by coming back to God in Christ Jesus, as we allow Him to cleanse us of everything that has been tampered with and changed because of sin, we see and understand that God's way will demand us to forsake our own way, because it absolutely profits nothing. We yield daily as God brings us to a place where we realize we are God's sons. It is His Spirit in us that qualifies us as sons, and our heart's cry at this amazing awareness can only be summed up in the phrase "Abba Father." This is where everything else falls into its respective place and God is known as the source of all things.

In our new and perfect image, we are completely satisfied in being a vessel of His Spirit in us. The difference is clear from when we had to inhabit our own bodies in error. In our total confusion and despair, separated from God by sin, it made sense to inhabit our own bodies and become slaves to our flesh while believing we were the masters of our own destiny. We weren't created to do that, so there has been a lot of distortion of our entire bodies, souls, minds, and everything that goes with them.

The Spirit of God in us corrects all that and resets us for life in Christ, our new and perfect image. It gets better. Not only are we sons; we have also been made heirs. In our error, we were considered slaves because of sin and our separation from God. We, like the prodigal son, were comfortable with eating leftovers from the pigs, a clear picture of how much sin limits, denies, and imprisons us, but all we need to do is go back home, ask for forgiveness, and receive a cleansing and new robes of righteousness. It is your right to live at home again. Your home is Christ Jesus. He is your true and perfect image.

"To whom God would make known what is the riches of the glory of this mystery among the Gentiles; which is Christ in you, the hope of glory" (Col. 1:27).

Christ in us is a concept that is a little intimidating for some believers, because some are yet to know how much God loves them and wants them to let Him be in their lives. Many are very comfortable with worshipping from a distance and going through the motions because of a certain awe they have of God as being too mighty to be approached. The truth is, even as mighty as He is, He created us within Christ Jesus for good works, so our original positioning is within Him and He in us. Apart from Him we can do nothing.

Our place on the inside of Christ is a place of complete dependency, both because of location and need. Our connection points for everything that pertains to life and godliness, and all forms of survival are directly of Him by design, so living apart or separated from Him isn't even a valid option.

Jesus has made a way for us to come all the way back to living in Him and having our being in Him; His life in us is the key that has unlocked our captivity to sin and has freed us to know what the riches of God's glory are. Christ in us as our life is our real and perfect image. It is another level of living that doesn't include the effects of the confined and regulated world human understanding presents. It isn't the circumstances that magically change; it is our understanding that is renewed to include the things that are freely given to us by God, which in turn shorten our list of needs. Christ Jesus is our perfect image.

"But as many as received him, to them gave he power to become the sons of God, even to them that believe on his name: Which were born, not of blood, nor of the will of the flesh, nor of the will of man, but of God" (John 1:12–13).

We've been given the right to become a child of God. Notice that we've been called the children of God; here we are given a right to "become" children of God. This is a gift that comes as a result of receiving Jesus. Yes, God created everyone, but you have a choice to be an active and productive child or just a self-absorbed prodigal.

You cannot have that gift any other way except to receive Him as Lord and believe in His name. You may wish hard for it, but you would get only whatever tricks your mind can play on you. The wonderful thing is that there is no discrimination here; anyone who truly believes gets it. The right to become His children is included as part of the package and must be received accordingly.

You who have received should be eternally grateful. Share your excitement and show others how to get this free gift. We need only to believe and receive Him. Pray a blessing on everyone who introduced Jesus Christ to you and all who have encouraged or continue to encourage you in your journey. Bless those whose actions, words, or the lack of them brought you closer to God in gratitude or desperation, for those were your growing moments, when you didn't even realize them.

God helps us to learn to be comfortable and confident in our position as His children. You always need to remember that what you seem to be outside of Christ is false, but what you are becoming in Jesus Christ is the real you. Make yourself available to God by depending on Him and trusting His guidance. Let your thoughts acknowledge His sovereignty at all times. As He nudges you by His Spirit, when you fall back into familiar thought patterns, quickly remember that real life is found only in Christ Jesus, your perfect image.

Lord, we thank You that You've made it possible for us to become fully yours. We trust You to finish the work You've started in us by bringing us to Your perfect image for Your glory in Jesus's name.

"And you hath he quickened, who were dead in trespasses and sins; wherein in time past ye walked according to the course of this world, according to the prince of the power of the air, the spirit that now worketh in the children of disobedience" (Eph. 2:1–2).

Our old image showed us as dead in our sins and unbelief. We manifested the deception we had received as truth and suffered the consequences of it. We accepted it because we weren't fully aware of the power of God's truth. Jesus is the truth, and His message of love changes our status from "dead" to "alive." The second verse is a clear description of our former mirror image. Thank God for His mercies; by Jesus Christ, our Savior, we have been quickened and now live in Him.

Truth overrides lies. Lies seem to make sense until truth comes along, and when we know the truth, no one wants to remember what the lies were. We are not our own; we were created to live and move and totally have our being in Him; any deviation from that plan allows for our weakness and defeat. The perfect cure for that isn't to continue to seek to be provided for in captivity; rather it is to realize that we have a home waiting for us and to go there. Christ is our home, our resting place, where we live and move. Our perfect image, our being, is found only in Him. We need to abandon everything and lay a full grip on this truth, for in it is the strength for our weakness, hope for our despair, joy for our sadness, and grace for our shortcomings. There is no time to waste. There are no earthly things that are as remotely important as this.

Father, we honor You for coming for us in Jesus, Your Son. Thank You for everything You did at Calvary and continue to do by Your Spirit in us.

Make us content to be Yours and Yours alone, because we're really not missing out on anything; rather, we're gaining life in You. In Jesus's name, amen.

"But now in Christ Jesus ye who sometimes were far off are made nigh by the blood of Christ. For he is our peace, who hath made both one, and hath broken down the middle wall of partition between us" (Eph. 2:13–14).

Sin is so loathsome to God that it separates us from Him, locks us out of His abundance, and keeps us far away. But God loves us so much that He allowed a part of Him, His Son, Jesus, to come as a man and touch sin and broken humanity, destroying its power by meeting its demands of death and rising again to demonstrate His power over sin and death. From far off, everything appears smaller and inaccessible because our understanding outside of Christ presents a distorted image of life, one that charges at us at every opportunity to expose our inability. Not anymore—Jesus has made the way.

Everyone can now come close. God isn't angry at us, His blood has atoned for us, and

He has obtained pardon and grace at every place of sin. He wants us to live in His peace and manifest His glory. Having lived away from His grace, we all understand the difference between far and near. To be far from God is to subscribe to the law of sin and death, but the law of the Spirit of life in Christ Jesus is what we are offered free of charge; we can now make full claims to live as God's children in all conduct and thought. We have been fully enabled to do so

It is a thing of joy to know we're not alone anymore and that Christ in us is greater than he who is in the world. This is the confidence we have when we choose to think of victory instead of fear. Our God doesn't fight wars; He conquers, because none can stand against Him. We can now live according to the original plan of God, our perfect image.

"For God hath not given us the spirit of fear; but of power, and of love, and of a sound mind" (2 Tim. 1:7).

Most believers in Christ know how to quote this verse, and it's probably a favorite verse for some. It's nice to know that God didn't give us a spirit of fear. Please read this again as information, not as a favorite Bible verse.

Imagine that you went to a store to pick up a gift that was prepurchased for you, but you were given a package that didn't quite seem like what you thought it would be. As you pondered what to do, the one who had bought the gift called you on the phone.

"I hope you like your new trendy outfit. It reminded me so much of you when I saw it, and I had to buy it for you."

You replied that you were given a box filled with girls' toys. "I didn't see any outfit," you added.

The person on the phone confidently declared

from a point of truth and authority, "I didn't buy you girls' toys. I bought you a silver-and-black-colored outfit with side pockets, and it was exactly your size!" I'm sure most of us wouldn't leave that place, no matter what reasons we were given, until we received the right gift that was purchased for us.

God, who made you, is the same One who keeps you. He says to you that He never gave you a spirit of fear, so refuse fear whenever it presents itself regardless of its reasons. Drop it and ask for what He did give you. This is your right from God at all times. Whenever you feel afraid, exchange that fear for God's power, His love, and a sound mind. Declare this truth within you or aloud. Make a conscious effort to move away from whatever images fear had painted in your imagination. Remember that what you fear is only as real as your focus and thought process on it. Allow God's peace to overtake you and establish His power, love, and sound mind. His Spirit in you is your help.

Practice it as often as the opportunity presents itself, and you will see a new awareness become part of you. As one who was given a spirit of power, love, and a sound mind, fear can no longer be part of you. Your perfect image doesn't include fear. Praise God.

"But ye shall receive power, after that the Holy Ghost is come upon you: and ye shall be witnesses unto me both in Jerusalem, and in all Judaea, and in Samaria, and unto the uttermost part of the earth" (Acts 1:8).

The Spirit of God is the life of God in us. We are powerless without Him, and there is no reason to be without power. The Holy Spirit is the enabler, according to the will of God, in our lives. He doesn't empower us for selfish gains or best-intentioned plans. He reveals only Christ and all He would do in us and through us. The burden of self-dependency is removed when the Holy Spirit empowers us. We are free to witness the amazing things He does in us and through us, and we can now gladly accept that we're not our own. He owns us as His temple.

This is the current human situation; we are always in need of power. We're unable to do most things by ourselves; that is why technology is a big help. Technology has allowed us to do more; it has given us that extra ability outside regular human capacity. There's no comparison here except in the inabilities the lack of power presents to any person, but we are unable to fully function to our God-ordained capacity without the Holy Spirit. This power isn't optional and is God's life within us. The absence of this power in our daily lives isn't to be desired. It deprives us of everything that pertains to life and godliness, and leaves us with only what our human understanding can muster up

It's important that we become fully aware of who the Spirit of God is on our behalf. In human terms, I would dare to compare Him rather loosely to the engine of a car. He is the central part of us, and our bodies are His temple. You probably have seen other things take over a human body, causing it to manifest accordingly. You may have seen how a person behaves under the influence of any substance that overpowers him or her. Alcohol, just a liquid, has the ability to completely redirect the mind and body of a whole human created in God's image.

The body was created for God's Spirit to inhabit. He is our seal and guarantee. Adjust your image today as you ask God to take over your life by His Spirit. Believe this and receive the power He brings to you.

"In whom are hid all the treasures of wisdom and knowledge" (Col. 2:3).

In Christ is hidden all the treasures of wisdom and knowledge. This truth is really hard to process, because we've been exposed to so many varying experiences in life that have conditioned our hearts and minds to fully accept limitations. We are very aware of what we can do and what is beyond our ability, and we use that to map out our lives. Armed with these boundaries, we set out to plan our lives and find whatever help we can to make life a little easier as we would understand that to be.

We realize we cannot fly, so we invent the airplane to do it for us, but the airplane isn't faultless. We write as a substitute for speech, and we use telephones and various other modern devices that help us bridge distances in conversation and visuals, but we still cannot touch or feel the person we're communicating with from a long distance, at least not yet.

I can barely imagine what would happen to our seeming limitations if we became more aware of the truth that all the treasures of wisdom and knowledge—everything—are really hidden in Christ. If all of it is hidden in Christ, that means there is no wisdom outside of Christ. If Christ lives in you, hidden within you are all the treasures of wisdom and knowledge. This doesn't need to make any more sense to you. It is the truth. I wonder what it would do to our mirror image when we learn by His Spirit to make full use of the wisdom in us through Christ and to question and compare every other so-called wisdom with this truth.

May we always choose the wisdom of Christ over man's wisdom, even when it seems to makes no sense, because You, Lord, are the ultimate wisdom that puts to shame whatever else seems wise. Father, open our hearts to this life-changing truth. Help us to remember with joy that within us is Your wisdom, and it isn't limited by any earthly laws. Our perfect image is complete in You. Blessed be Your name, in Jesus's name.

"And having spoiled principalities and powers, he made a shew of them openly, triumphing over them in it" (Col. 2:15).

Well, it doesn't look like principalities and powers are spoiled, judging by all the troubles we face daily, even as Christians. The punishment for sin is death and eternal separation from God in heaven and on earth. God extended Himself in Jesus Christ, His Son, and reached down into the muck and mire of man's sin to pull him out, cleanse him, and restore him unto Himself. Principalities and powers are the different entities and levels of deception, strongholds, and platforms that give sin its power over the human mind and use this as a base to infest everything in a person's life. These had to be disarmed to rescue us from their grip and set us free. With His shed blood and His broken body, with His death and resurrection, Jesus made full payment for our sins, thus breaking every chain that held us captive.

It is necessary that we know this as we continue in our walk with God. If we are fully aware of the fact that our captivity has been held captive, we would be more confident in our everyday life; we would ignore the threats of these same disarmed authorities and powers in our lives, because the only power they have over us now is our belief in their capability. They have been disarmed, and until we let God help us by His Spirit to know this truth and use it to replace any lie that opposes it, we will continually need to fight these powers instead of only resisting them as they try to deceive us.

It is God's will that we believe Him. It is our only truth; everything else just isn't true. Father, what we need more than anything is to believe You. You are all You say You are, and You've done all You say You did. To doubt You would be to put You in the same category as a mere human and find You wanting. You are God, and in You everything has its source.

Help us to correct our image and receive the real life Your victory has given us. In Jesus's name, amen.

"That your faith should not stand in the wisdom of men, but in the power of God" (1 Cor. 2:5).

This is quite a clear-cut instruction that changes everything. Paul identified the source of his preaching as the power of God, not his own wisdom or eloquence. Sometimes I am amazed at how directly God's Word applies to our lives. Here two different sources present two opinions; one is true, and one is false. In His love, God tells us exactly which one to believe. In a world built and dominated by human wisdom, nothing else makes sense, yet the power of God has no alternatives. The wisdom of man cannot be compared to the all-consuming knowledge of the One who made all things and in whom all things hold together.

Is your faith based on the conditions you face, or is it based on the power of God, who can do anything? The worst situation any human can imagine or dream cannot hinder Him. If the weatherman forecasts a devastating storm, we naturally get worried and make plans for safety. It's the right thing to do, but I'm always reminded of Jesus sleeping in a boat that filled up with water on a dreadful stormy night. There is room to believe more because that has already been demonstrated as a possibility. Everything Jesus did was an example of what we have been given power to do in a normal setting. He even added that we can do more because the Father by His Spirit gives us help.

I understand that we are called to live according to a very different set of rules, and our victory is found when we choose to ignore what we know and believe God, who made it all. Believing God is strange and may make you lose many fake people and earthly things, but would you rather be powerless in the midst of such abundance of power and love God has released to you, the believer? May our faith always rest on the power of God, and may the wisdom of men never take us captive, in Jesus's name. Our perfect image is one with authority.

"Blessed be the God and Father of our Lord Jesus Christ, who hath blessed us with all spiritual blessings in heavenly places in Christ" (Eph. 1:3).

Sometimes when I read certain Bible passages again after some time, I wonder aloud whether they have always been here. As I grow in Christ, the Bible continues to become a mine of endless blessings for here, now, and forever.

We have been blessed with every spiritual blessing in the heavenly realm. Pause on that thought for a while and let your entire being make an effort to believe it. It's true. If you are like me, you suddenly feel deprived because you just discovered this fact. His Spirit reminds me when a verse becomes clearer to me, I hear within me, "It has always been in that book." Why did I just become aware of this? The answer is found in obedience. No guilt is allowed here, only solutions, because we need to make full use of all we have in Christ. The answer is ours.

This is how I deal with this: The verse is true because God is true. It has no human limitation attached to it. What is left to do is to obey. I then realize how unable I am to do that, but I want what it gives. This is where I always break into praise; I have been given a helper too. Ask and receive the help.

God's Spirit helps us every step of the way; He directs and redirects, nudges, and admonishes. He gives whatever is needed to bring us to the attainment of this free gift of God. The journey can be short if we learn to keep our eyes on the mark. Distractions cannot stop us; we live to win. We are undefeatable in Christ. Sin shall not dwell in our mortal bodies; it cannot. Abandon it, ask, and use the forgiveness He provided at Calvary. And we push on for His glory in all manner of His righteousness.

Get back up again and go. Get excited enough about this fact: every spiritual blessing in the heavenly realm is yours. You really can have it and keep it too but only by His Spirit. Just imagine whom you would have become if you'd learned to walk fully in these gifts; they are yours. God desires you to have them in reality. That is your perfect image.

"And that ye put on the new man, which after God is created in righteousness and true holiness" (Eph. 4:24).

The reality of who we are or have always been is found only when we are renewed in the spirit of our minds. We were created according to God in true righteousness and holiness, and that fact has never changed at any time. Nothing has the ability to negate that truth about us. The only thing that happened is that our minds became darkened and confused because of sin, and we couldn't see ourselves past the form of a regular mirror.

It is necessary to take time out and express profound gratitude for this great grace and mercy toward such formerly undeserving people like us. God has now qualified us by forgiving us and covering us with His righteousness; He hides us in Him and continues to cleanse and renew us to bring us to the new self-image, which was actually our only image when we were created in the image of God. The revelation of what we could be encourages us to push forward, yield more, become more patient, forgive, and just count it all joy, because we now realize that the destination is the reclaiming of our real self in Christ. This is a new and necessary experience for us after we have been lost for so long and have fully accepted the lie that we are less than who God created us to be in Him.

This verse gives a clear description of our real image: the new man, created after God in righteousness and true holiness. May we receive new excitement about who we could be when we let Him renew us and celebrate the truth about our real image in Him.

"Ye have not chosen me, but I have chosen you, and ordained you, that ye should go and bring forth fruit, and that your fruit should remain: that whatsoever ye shall ask of the Father in my name, he may give it you" (John 15:16).

Any doubts that may have tampered with our true image in Christ don't stand a chance in light of this truth. He chose us. He also appointed us. There always was a specific reason for our existence, and that is the only truth about who we are. Let the love that the words *chosen*, and *ordained* convey calm you and position you properly in Him. This isn't a lucky pick; we were destined and specifically appointed and equipped for the work we would do. Living outside this knowledge or only believing some of it denies us what is rightfully ours and denies the world of what your purpose is.

We do have a life, a plan, and an original design. Our story is false or at best incomplete without this truth properly embedded in us;

whatever else we know and think of ourselves needs to be corrected. Now we need to focus on our reasons for being here; we should go and bear fruit, and our fruit should remain. This among other things refers to the growth that happens after we have found our true and correct foundation: our real and perfect image. There would be no fruit if we didn't take root at our designed location and yield to the master in all conditions; in full knowledge that He is keeping us, and that we surely shall bear fruit according to His purpose.

I pray that the confidence and security of this truth will fill us with joy, as we cast the burden of our lives unto Him, and live as those who are chosen and appointed to go and bear fruit. His life in us will sustain our fruit.

"Ye are all the children of light, and the children of the day: we are not of the night, nor of darkness" (1 Thess. 5:5).

The line is drawn between light and darkness, and we have been included in the light. Once, we weren't aware of which side we were on, because in error we believed and acted wrongly; we neglected God's life within us and chose to suffer the consequences of sin. In His love, God continues to shed the light of His truth on us through His Word, using every possible way to convince us of His love, care, and His never-ending pursuit of us.

Since we have now been able by His grace to eliminate what we are not, let us concentrate on what we are, because that is our true and correct image. It is who we are, and we should move forward confidently, not leaving any room for deception as we did in the past. We should have nothing to do with things of darkness or the night. The reference here is to anything that doesn't keep us in God's light. It is important to remember that it is never beneficial as children of the light to stay in the dark. When your entire being, which is designed to thrive in the light, is positioned in the dark, it won't thrive. It will be misused because whatever the light offers cannot be truly manifested when the vessel surrenders to the dark.

Let this truth become a compass that leads us wherever we may find ourselves in our walk of life. May we always remember that as sons and daughters of light, we have nothing to do with the kingdom of darkness but to illuminate it with our light.

"But ye are a chosen generation, a royal priesthood, an holy nation, a peculiar people; that ye should shew forth the praises of him who hath called you out of darkness into his marvellous light" (1 Peter 2:9).

This is one of those passages that continues to decorate our image in Him and gives us the confidence to live out the life that is ours by original design. This life was made available to us again by the sacrifice of Jesus on the cross. Many are only inspired at best when they read these verses, because they can barely relate to them. But we aren't asked to relate to them; we are asked to believe them because the One who made all things has designed that we believe them to experience the blessings and enabling that they offer.

Let us think on these words: "chosen generation," "royal priesthood," "holy nation," and "special or peculiar people." These words cannot be retracted; they are waiting for us to leave every lie we have believed, to forsake all the logic that had us bound to these lies, and to hold onto the truth, even if it makes absolutely no sense to us. Whenever the option is between what you know and can make sense of and what God says of you, even when it makes no sense to you, the correct choice is always to go with God by the help of His Spirit. Just say what God says of you back to Him, call yourself what He calls you, and try what He says you can do. It is His power and His Word, and the only things that can stop you are the old road maps of deception, which continue to sabotage your thoughts. Each of these accolades is a position through which His praise will be shown.

Praises to Him who loved us enough not to leave us in darkness, the One whose light dispels all forms or suggestions of darkness, including its shadows, memories, and fake comfort zones. He has called us out into His marvelous light, and this is our true and perfect form.

"Put on therefore, as the elect of God, holy and beloved, bowels of mercies, kindness, humbleness of mind, meekness, longsuffering" (Col. 3:12).

Sometimes when we look at the responsibility that goes with our true image, it is possible to become discouraged and feel inadequate. Many people give up and become satisfied with just doing the things of God. The virtues listed above can be birthed in us only by His Spirit, so there is no need to feel intimidated and try by our might to put on tender mercies, kindness, humility, meekness, and long-suffering. These become fake and grossly ineffective when they are by-products of our human understanding or efforts

Our true image is a lifestyle; it is the total package of all that makes up who we are for His kingdom purposes. God created us as His temples so He would live in us by His Spirit. We don't have a legitimate life or order of events that are outside Him. He is the power in us, so when we live in our true image, we are everything we are supposed to be, and we have all the ability that is available to us. Truly the promises of God and the blessings of God are attainable here on earth just as Jesus demonstrated when He walked on earth. We are fully equipped by His righteousness over us to live in victory, and His Spirit renews our minds and releases wisdom for every seeming difficulty. We have the ability to love as Christ loves and to share His love. God's Spirit in us works this love out in our perfect image in Him.

We believe fully that with God nothing shall be impossible; our human minds can make sense of this fact because God created all things, and in Him, in His Son, Jesus, our Savior, all things consist. All those of creation stand at their respective posts in His presence.

It is important for us to discard any idea or thought that identifies us without Christ,

Rosalyn U. Ikpatt

because that is what keeps us tethered to the lies that defined us for so long. We are free to be and do all God demands of us in our new and perfect image.

"Study to shew thyself approved unto God, a workman that needeth not to be ashamed, rightly dividing the word of truth" (2 Tim. 2:1).

Our true life is a continuous journey and must be diligently maintained lest we get tricked to fall back into the deception that had us bound and still binds the world. Everything in Christ is a gift and is available but must be recognized, received, and kept in our hearts. We must realize our overwhelming need for God in His Spirit to inhabit us, for we are lost without Him. With this realization come gratitude and a fervent yielding, because we know what we need and how much better we can be with that help.

The Word of God is readily available for us to read; we should always read it prayerfully and ask for guidance. As we study His Word, we're able to know more about the heart of God, and it is the receiving of that love that stabilizes us. It is dangerous to run this race of life without Christ in our consciousness and memories. We had lived it, and the difference is clear; we refuse to navigate this maze of deception without the help God has appointed for us, His Spirit in us.

The truth that God loves us and wouldn't wish for anyone to perish is demonstrated as often as necessary in the Bible. It is presented in forms tailored for varying personality types, but the message stays the same. God has made provision for the sins that stood against us in His presence. He has put them on Christ Jesus and destroyed them. We don't need to deal with those sins anymore. The Word opens wisdom and knowledge up for us in specific ways according to what God is doing in us, even as we study them.

We're able to receive His forgiveness and move back to life in Christ, which was His real and only purpose for us. Here our lives are anchored and rooted in Christ, and we have no direct contact with the cares of the world.

Christ is our covering and our shock absorber; when we become used to living in Him, the burden of life rolls off us and frees us up to be able to see with the eyes of our hearts. This is different from what we see with eyes that only understand sin and the consequences of it. Our perfect image restores and heals us; it establishes God's kingdom in and through us as we diligently study His Word.

"Set your affection on things above, not on things on the earth. For ye are dead, and your life is hid with Christ in God" (Col. 3:2–3).

The Bible continues to build our perfect image in us piece by piece as we let His Spirit work His Word out in us. Here we are given shortcuts around the influx of information, issues, and situations that beg for our attention at every passing moment. We are given clear and precise instructions on what to focus on, which would leave everything else irrelevant to our spiritual journey. I couldn't help but notice that this concentration on good and wholesome thoughts has the ability to move us from a place of despair to one of hope.

I compare our regular unchecked thought patterns to those that are intentional and belief based, and I observe that the thoughts His Word recommends activate His promises and everything we need for life and godliness. This way of thinking is the correct way our prayers are answered. God is a holy God, and He works in holiness. His counsels don't include man-made solutions and coping methods. He wants us to totally forsake our former ways of life and just listen and obey His words as He leads us out of a place of deception and insufficiency to a place of abundance of everything good.

Many may argue that suffering and pain are part of life, but being helpless and overwhelmed isn't an option. We have grace for every situation when we set our minds on things not on earth, and until we use it, we will be denied the things it presents to us. A very wealthy person may be inconvenienced because he or she runs out of groceries and needs to go shopping, but his or her inconvenience isn't to be compared to someone who has no groceries and doesn't have the means to get them. We receive from wherever we look for help, and the best place to look is to your maker, who has a flawless track record in loving us. We don't need to allow certain issues to become normal in our lives; we have help. Set your mind on Christ, submit to Him, resist the Enemy, and he will flee from you. That is our normal perfect image in Christ.

"Know ye not that ye are the temple of God, and that the Spirit of God dwelleth in you" (1 Cor. 3:16).

Our perfect image is Christ in us; by His Spirit, we are His temple. To be His temple, we must remember that we were created for God to inhabit. We were made in His image, shaped to contain Him in a specific way, but sin dictated that we neglect that truth and live independently of God or at best worship Him from a distance while denying ourselves His ever-present help.

I like the way this verse is, a question, almost like a stern reminder; it is easy to believe that we can function independently of God's Spirit. Everything tells us we can, and technology continues to invent new ways to manage our self-dependency. Most societies encourage self-dependency because the knowledge of God in Christ Jesus and His relationship with human beings aren't completely understood or just aren't a priority. As a result, it makes perfect sense to live your life anyway it pleases you, because you believe your life is your own. The believer in Christ, however, knows he or she is a created being, made to contain the life of God for His purposes and not for his or her very limited and often-ignorant reasons.

Since our bodies are the temples of God, we must make room for Him. We must let Him empty this temple, remove everything that doesn't belong, and reset it to its original coordinates for Him. This sounds like a great sacrifice we need to make for God at our own expense, but it is truly the only and proper use of our bodies; whatever loss we encounter here is no loss at all, because whatever cannot be included in our lives in Christ isn't necessary. We should be grateful. Until we realize our only duty is to yield God's temple, our bodies, as a living sacrifice to Him, the error of sin and self-dependency will continue to entice us.

We have no authority to use our bodies for anything else but total submission to God, through whom we would find wisdom and strength to have proper and God-honoring lives and relationships. Our true image is a yielded temple where His Spirit dwells, provides, cares for us, and enables the temple within in every good way while manifesting the victorious Christ.

"Yet Nay, in all these things we are more than conquerors through him that loved us. For I am persuaded, that neither death, nor life, nor angels, nor principalities, nor powers, nor things present, nor things to come, Nor height, nor depth, nor any other creature, shall be able to separate us from the love of God, which is in Christ Jesus our Lord" (Rom. 8:37–39).

What an inspiring declaration! It gladdens our minds to know we are so covered by God's love that none of those things we are terrified of can disconnect us from His love. The passage goes on to say something that sounds so far from our present reality: that we are more than conquerors. When we look at our lives and circumstances, we see that we are defeated more than we have conquered. This fact makes us wonder whether the Word of God is true or just inspiring.

This is a good place for us to observe the difference between our real and true image in Christ and the lies we have believed. These declarations are true, and we are enabled in Christ, who is our only and perfect image. The only obstacle standing in our way is unbelief. There is no reason for unbelief, but it has many claims on our minds and thoughts. We must believe that Jesus took our inabilities along when He took our sins on Himself on the cross. Can you imagine us being so convinced of God's love that we don't cower in the face of these things? God says of us that we are more than conquerors.

I think it's time to hover our minds over these verses that specifically tell us who and what we are and can do. The way to believe is to ask for help from His Holy Spirit in us. The above verses reveal our true image and encourage us to press on to become our true and real selves in Christ, in whom we were created. God addresses us in our true forms and continues to present us a way to come back to who we really are, our true image.

"In whom we have redemption through his blood, the forgiveness of sins, according to the riches of his grace" (Eph. 1:7).

By God's grace and through the sacrifice Jesus made on the cross, we have been forgiven and released from the consequences of sin and death. We must ask and receive help from His Spirit to discontinue any belief systems that were or are opposed to God and His ways. The subtle ones are the most troublesome ones. We must be willing to fully allow God's Spirit to remove from our lives those things that seem right but don't work the works of God or His kingdom. The cloaks of deception and all their desires and compulsions are over. In Christ, however, we have a completely different identity, and this is our true image, which is being revealed.

We must consciously embrace the new life of redemption we have been given with overwhelming gratefulness. Think about it for a minute. What if we were still held captive in the futility of our minds? What if we were still waiting for some grand event outside of God's will to convince us of His love?

Right here, at this very moment, God has justified you. He has taken on Himself your sins and the consequences that were due to you because of sin. His sacrifice on your behalf has been accepted and duly processed, so you must speak what God speaks concerning you. The laws have changed, because Christ lives in you now. They cannot be the same again. Your ability to live in Him isn't needed; you need only to allow Him to work His works in you.

Realize that life can no longer start with your reasoning or understanding of cause and effect. It has to start with Him and flow through you. Let your thoughts be based on His truth, and everything else will correct itself. It all has to happen within Christ to be true. Correct your image accordingly. There is life in Christ, and you have your being in Him.

The revelation of Jesus Christ, our Savior:

It is important to refresh our minds all over again of the reason behind our hope. Jesus is also the author and finisher of our faith. If you are a believer in God through the Lord Jesus Christ by His Spirit and have made Him Lord of your life, allow your mind to come alive again and rejoice in these truths of His wonderful love for you as you read these.

If you're not yet a believer but are curious about the things of God, you can become part of this amazing love. Please read on. Everything in this book is for information and practical use. God is always pulling you to Himself, and this could be a great time for your destiny to change for good.

The testimony of Jesus as God and man:

In whom we have redemption through his blood, even the forgiveness of sins: Who is the image of the invisible God, the firstborn of every creature: For by him were all things created, that are in heaven, and that are in earth, visible and invisible, whether they be thrones, or dominions, or principalities, or powers: all things were created by him, and for him: And he is before all things, and by him all things consist. And he is the head of the body, the church: who is the beginning, the firstborn from the dead; that in all things he might have the preeminence. For it pleased the Father that in him should all fulness dwell; And, having made peace through the blood of his cross, by him to reconcile all things unto himself; by him, I say, whether they be things in earth, or things in heaven. And you, that were sometime alienated and enemies in your mind by wicked works, yet now hath he reconciled. In the body of his flesh through death, to present you holy and unblameable and unreproveable in his sight. (Col. 1:14–22)

The Bible verses above clearly explain who Jesus is and why He died for us. They are specifically worded to cover all the physical and spiritual questions as well as God questions. Here Jesus is introduced as the extension of God, the image of the invisible God; in Him dwells all the fullness of God. He is the Word used to create the world, because by Him all things were created, and all things imaginable were made. By Him, for Him, through Him, and in Him they consist. That leaves nothing out.

He is the One who took our place, died on the cross, took the full punishment for our sins, and rose again to bring us back into a full union with God in Him. We need to continue in the faith without wavering or distraction to reap the full benefits of our redemption. Our true image is in Him.

John introduced Jesus and His ministry:

There was a man sent from God, whose name was John. The same came for a witness, to bear witness of the Light, that all men through him might believe. He was not that Light, but was sent to bear witness of that Light. That was the true Light, which lighteth every man that cometh into the world. He was in the world, and the world was made by him, and the world knew him not. He came unto his own, and his own received him not. But as many as received him, to them gave he power to become the sons of God, even to them that believe on his name: Which were born, not of blood, nor of the will of the flesh, nor of the will of man, but of God. And the Word was made flesh, and dwelt among us, (and we beheld his glory, the glory as of the only begotten of the Father,) full of grace and truth. John bare witness of him, and cried, saying, This was he of whom I spake, He that cometh after me is preferred before me: for he was before me. And of his fulness have all we received, and grace for grace. For the law was given by Moses, but grace and truth came by Jesus Christ. No man hath seen God at any time, the only begotten Son, which is in the bosom of the Father, he hath declared him. (John 1:6–18)

John was sent as a witness, to help us receive Christ Jesus as who He really is, and not just pass Him off as any ordinary prophet or miracle worker, thereby missing our true lives in Him. The spectacular mission of redemption needed to be made known in every possible way. God's heart is shown in how far He would go to send an announcer, a witness, a forerunner to set the pace for His plan of love for us. Again here we see Christ as our life, and we are blessed to be in Him, for we are truly complete in Him. The law came through Moses, but Jesus, the Light of the World, the extension of God, and the image of the invisible God, brings us truth and grace.

The amazing testimony of Mary, the mother of Jesus:

"His mother saith unto the servants, Whatsoever he saith unto you, do it" (John 2:5).

This is one of the most profound statements said about Jesus from a woman who had a front row seat to the spiritual beginnings of Jesus's earthly life. She always knew His word was powerful, and she never interfered with His mission. That advice echoes through even today; we would do well to do whatever He says. Like in this story of the wedding at Cana, described in the verse above, when the servants did what Jesus said to do as Mary suggested, there was a manifestation of His power in supernatural ways. The same is true today. Our perfect image in Him is made alive in obedience.

The Father testifies of Jesus:

> And Jesus, when he was baptized, went up straightway out of the water: and, lo, the heavens were opened unto him, and he saw the Spirit of God descending like a dove, and lighting upon him: And lo a voice from heaven, saying, This is my beloved Son, in whom I am well pleased. (Matt. 3:16–17)

> While he yet spake, behold, a bright cloud overshadowed them: and behold a voice out of the cloud, which said, This is my beloved Son, in whom I am well pleased; hear ye him. And when the disciples heard it, they fell on their face, and were sore afraid. And Jesus came and touched them, and said, Arise, and be not afraid. And when they

had lifted up their eyes, they saw no
man, save Jesus only. (Matt. 17:5–8)

That is the final authority, the endorsement
of the Most High God. Again, these verses don't
need any extra explanation. The display of the
power of God here is shown in the opening
of the heavens, the bright clouds, the dove,
and the voice. The life and natural forms only
confirmed His sovereignty: Jesus, the Son of
God, our Savior, the image of the invisible God,
the One in whom we have our true image.

Peter shared his revelation of Jesus:

> And Simon Peter answered and said, Thou art the Christ, the Son of the living God. And Jesus answered and said unto him, Blessed art thou, Simon Barjona: for flesh and blood hath not revealed it unto thee, but my Father which is in heaven. (Matt. 16:16–17)

> Neither is there salvation in any other: for there is none other name under heaven given among men, whereby we must be saved. (Acts 4:12)

Jesus is the way, the truth, and the life. In Him all of creation holds together. He isn't a brand of religion; He is the light that lights every man's path, and He has provided salvation for anyone from any background who will believe in Him. These are just a few reminders among uncountable testimonies of our Savior, Jesus Christ. This truth will set anyone free if he or she really wants it. You need to know Him, believe in Him, and accept His words as true. You must receive His sacrifice on the cross as full payment for every sin in your life. Forgiveness and cleansing are free gifts He gives you. You must get to know Him closely and commune with Him daily as He reveals Himself in you by His Spirit. His desire is for you to come out and live completely in Him and through Him—not as an option or when needed but because it was, and will always be, His only plan for you.

If you don't know Him or are yet to find your relationship with Him worthy of forsaking all else, then you need to know He hasn't given up on you. He is ever waiting for you to come home and learn again how to live as a child, not as a burdened slave of lies. There is no reason to delay; the struggles of life outside Christ are unnecessary. He has made everything possible in every way so you could always see and live out the correct image in your perfect mirror.

The testimony of Jesus in His own words:

> I can of mine own self do nothing:
> as I hear, I judge: and my judgment
> is just; because I seek not mine
> own will, but the will of the Father
> which hath sent me. If I bear
> witness of myself, my witness is not
> true. There is another that beareth
> witness of me; and I know that the
> witness which he witnesseth of me
> is true. Ye sent unto John, and he
> bare witness unto the truth. But I
> receive not testimony from man:
> but these things I say, that ye might
> be saved. He was a burning and a
> shining light: and ye were willing
> for a season to rejoice in his light.
> But I have greater witness than that
> of John: for the works which the
> Father hath given me to finish, the
> same works that I do, bear witness

of me, that the Father hath sent me. And the Father himself, which hath sent me, hath borne witness of me. Ye have neither heard his voice at any time, nor seen his shape. And ye have not his word abiding in you: for whom he hath sent, him ye believe not. Search the scriptures; for in them ye think ye have eternal life: and they are they which testify of me. And ye will not come to me, that ye might have life. I receive not honour from men. (John 5:30–41)

Jesus, our Savior, King of Kings, and Lord of Lords, was presented as a mere man, who made an effort to convince religion-hardened people that He was the help they expected, but even the miracles didn't convince them. It is a sad occasion to receive the deliverance you need and yet be completely blind to it and sometimes even deceived into fighting to defend your opinion. God's grace and mercy are so great, for He has every reason to have given up on us long ago and even today. But not only did Jesus die and rise again for our sins, extending total forgiveness and cleansing to any who would accept them; God continues to keep and indwell us by His Spirit, providing everything to us that pertains to life and godliness. Read your Bible with a grateful heart. Our God really is good, and He really cares. Our perfect image in Him is His heart's desire for us; it is also our perfect life.

Printed in the United States
By Bookmasters